AF278898

PASSPORT TO GREATNESS

Upscale Your Potential for Success and Achievement

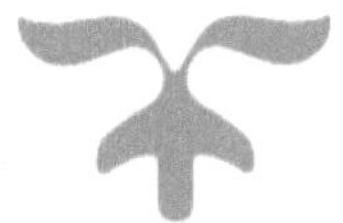

PASSPORT TO GREATNESS

Upscale Your Potential for Success and Achievement

Tim Anton Okhai

Passport to Greatness
Copyright © 2019 by Tim Anton Okhai
First Edition, First Impression,

ISBN: 978-0-9870-1637-9

Unless otherwise indicated, all Scripture quotations are from The Holy Bible, Authorised King James Version. Copyright 1962, by American Bible Society. Used by permission.

All Scripture quotations marked (NKJV) are from the New King James Version. Copyright 1979, 1980, 1982, by Thomas Nelson, Inc. Used by permission. All rights reserved.

All Scripture quotations marked (Amp.) are from the Amplified Bible, Expanded Edition. Copyright 1987 by The Zondervan Corporation and the Lockman Foundation. Used by permission. All rights reserved.

All Scripture quotations marked (The Book) are from Tyndale House Publishers Inc.

All rights reserved, no part of this publication may be reproduced, stored in a retrieval system or transmitted in any form or by any means, electronic, mechanical, photocopying, recording, or otherwise, without the prior written permission of the copyright owner.

Layout and Design: Truth House Publishing
Published by Passport to Greatness Media
For feedback and comments, contact:
WhatsApp: +27 745 199 419
E-mail: passporttogreatness@yahoo.com

ACKNOWLEDGEMENTS

This book owes its completion to the encouragement and support received from many different people along the way.

First, I owe an eternal debt of gratitude to my wife, Bertha, for standing by me throughout this journey, and provided the needed support, encouragement and enabling environment to complete this book. Thank you to our daughter, Praise, whose constant supply of tea and coffee stimulated my creativity and provided the needed boost to keep writing. I also wish to acknowledge Pastor Michel, whose regular prayers, guidance and encouragement kept me going when times were tough and the going was rough.

For the development and production of this book itself, I feel a deep sense of gratitude to the following persons:

Thanks to Nancy McHugh and Ebele Orakpo for their painstaking work in editing this book. Thanks to Alaythea Hamlyn for the formatting and layout, and for the feedback and suggestions that led to improvements in this book.

Several individuals read earlier versions of this book and provided helpful feedback and advice: Dr. Stephanie Moss and Lindsey Miller all deserve a hearty thank you.

I am grateful to all the writers, teachers, and mentors whose works, words and wisdom have shaped my life and thoughts, and stirred within me gifts that have made me who I am. Thank you for allowing me to share with you my thoughts and the lessons I've learned in life. Most of all, I am grateful to God for the creative ingenuity with which I was designed, and for the unique sets of gifts and talents with which I was dispatched to my generation.

You don't have to be great to get started.
But you have to get started to be great.

Les Brown

TABLE OF CONTENTS

INTRODUCTION

What is it that makes one man march forward all his life, conquering, accomplishing, and capturing his dreams – while another man never gets started?

Have you ever wondered what it is that gives one person such power, enthusiasm, and confidence that he or she can do things, but leaves another ineffectual and self-defeated?

What quality – if that is what we may call it – makes certain people able to see their way through any problem or handicap, find their path over all the rough spots of life to the fulfilment of their fondest dreams, while others struggle, fail, and despair?

You want to achieve your life's ambition and make all your dreams come true, don't you? Everybody does! Then why do so many people fail? Could it be that those who fail and remain in that state have never utilised – or even as much as recognised – the tremendous success-potential we all are born with? The more we learn to recognise it, believe in it, open ourselves to it and summon it to our aid, the more we find that goals are achieved, dreams are realised, high energy levels are attained and maintained, a greater degree of confidence and enthusiasm is developed, and a growing and fruitful life is not just possible, but almost inevitable?

I have spent years pondering these questions, researching, observing people, and reading all the self-help and motivational material that I can lay my hands on. By analysing the key principles of what I found and connecting the dots together, certain clues stand out very prominently, and these are the secrets that I share in this book. God has given to everyone a purpose in life, that is, to reach his or her maximum potential and become everything that he or she was created and gifted to be. To know, accept, and appreciate this is to have true peace and effortless triumph over the challenges of life; to ignore and neglect it is to struggle and fail.

Passport to Greatness will help you discover, develop, and put to use what makes you unique and special as an individual, and will also help you to upscale your potential for maximum success and achievement. To get the most out of this book, I recommend that you not only read it more than once, but that you complete the application exercise at the end of each chapter before moving on to the next chapter. If you do, your life will never be the same again by the time you finish reading the last chapter.

This book was not written in a hurry. It has been the culmination of wisdom distilled from over 25 years of observation, studies, and personal experience, encapsulated in one volume. So long as you are truly willing and committed to changing your life and your circumstances, I am confident that *Passport to Greatness* will strangle to death any entrenched pattern of negative self-image, will renew your confidence, and will give you fresh courage and hope to face the multi-faceted challenges of life with renewed vigour and zest. It will also unlock the door to the realisation of your dearest dreams and the steady, assured development of all your neglected but dynamic potential.

I wish I could tell you that this book was written by someone who had everything handed down to him on a silver platter. Sorry to disappoint; it wasn't. It was written by someone who, like most people, struggled with life's many options, choices, challenges, and storms. This book is a testimony that you don't have to have been born with privileges to succeed. Even a beginner can make his mark if he dares to try, to discover, to develop, and to put his unique set of abilities and talents to use. *Passport to Greatness* will liberate you from the ancient shackles of procrastination and it will confront the limiting mindset that you may have towards being an expert and starting to achieve. Most times, the right mental attitude – the 'I CAN DO THIS' attitude – is all it takes.

Wherever you are, or at whatever stage you are in your life right now, it is not too late to discover the real you – the person God created you to be. This book is a book of hope and expectation that will guide and help you to that place of discovery, growth, and the development of your innate abilities. My desire is that this book will clear the thick, dark cloud that stands between you and your goal, rescue you from the quicksand of negative self-image, failure, and despondency where you may be stuck, and help you to step courageously upon the first or next rung on your ladder to success and achievement.

Tim Anton Okhai
timokhai@yahoo.co.uk

Chapter One

DISCOVERING THE REAL YOU

But ye are a chosen generation, a royal priesthood,
a holy nation, a peculiar people; that ye should show
forth the praises of him who hath called you out of
darkness into his marvellous light.
1 Peter 2:9

To many a man, the real self is hidden behind a veil, unknown, undiscovered. The unveiling of the real you is critical to cultivating a healthy, positive self-image and to building a sense of inner worth founded upon a proper scriptural perspective. That is, in part, what this book seeks to accomplish – to lift this veil and bring you face-to-face with the real you: your worth, your potential.

The real you is custom-built, created to be unique in every way. The real you is not just the external, physical you that we see. Oh no, you are much more than what we see on the outside. The real you has nothing to do with your height, weight, or skin colour. The real you is internal, wonderful, and specially created by God to fit into a special place in creation. The real you is unique, special, creative, and priceless.

You are more than meets the eye. But you cannot be greater than the YOU you know you are. ***What you think you are is what you will become!*** (Proverbs 23:7)

Because of your worth, God took time to make everything about you special and wonderful. When the veil was lifted before him and he came face-to-face with his real self, David, in Psalm 139:14 exclaimed, *I will praise thee; for I am fearfully and wonderfully made: marvelous are thy works; and that my soul knoweth right well.*

Yes. David came to a point where, in his innermost being, he became fully aware, without a shadow of a doubt, how wonderfully and intricately he was crafted by God. Your uniqueness is underlined by the fact that, of the over seven billion people in the world today, no one is exactly like you. Similar in many ways, yes, but not exactly the same. After God made you, He destroyed the mould so that there can never be another you. Your life counts before God, and He believes in you so much that He has invested in you special abilities, gifts, and talents to help you manifest your greatness in life. In the eyes of men, you may be nothing special. But hold your shoulders high because in the sight of God, you are very special, valuable, and greatly loved, just the way you are. Men may look at you and classify you as weak, ugly, sickly, or unimportant, but the real you is wonderful, special, healthy, and strong. The opinion of men about you is not half as important as what God says about you, and what you say of yourself. Build a healthy self-image. Ignore all negative comments about you. Start saying something positive out loud about yourself today.

When men look at you, they judge you as you presently are. But when God looks at you, He sees you as you could become. He sees potential. He sees your future as He has planned it to be based on the gifts and talents He has deposited in you. That is why He chose an ordinary shepherd boy as king of Israel at a time when even his parents and siblings failed to see anything of worth and value in him. Each time they looked at him, all they saw was a little shepherd boy. But when God looked at him, He saw greatness in this little boy who would later become one of the greatest kings in Israel. Maybe that's why J W von Goethe once said, *Look at a man the way that he is, and he only becomes worse. But look at him as if he were what he could be, then he becomes what he should be.*

God has a special plan for your life that only you can fulfil. What's more, He has given you all you need to fulfil that plan – discover it! Not only that, history has a blank page reserved for you. Whatever you are able to accomplish in your lifetime goes down in the pages of history. Only you can fill your page in history; no one else can do it for you. You are peculiar because you have a unique part to play in the fulfilment of God's master plan in creation. Only you can deliver the package that you have been sent to this planet to deliver to your generation.

Hear me! God did not put you on planet earth just to exist. He created you and put you here to live a meaningful, purposeful, superabundant life. He created you to accomplish a specific mission on this earth, to return to Him with a detailed report of your life's activity, and to give a full account of what you have done with all the treasures and creative abilities He invested in you. It would be a tragedy not to discover your mission on earth. The day you discover your purpose for living, that is the day you stop merely existing and start really living, whether you are 18 or 81.

The Instinct To Win

The Weaver bird has never been to weaving school. But it can weave like a pro. The Canary has never enrolled in any music school. But when it opens its beak to sing, it cannot be ignored. The sperm does not have a GPS or physical map. But it knows exactly where to find the egg.

From the time of conception, you were programmed with the natural instinct to win. Millions of sperms competed for life, but one triumphed over them all, fertilised the egg and went ahead towards life. The resultant embryo that became you overcame many odds till finally you were born. So, you have been a winner from the beginning and God intends you to remain that way. You have not come this far only to end up in a garbage bin. You lived for a purpose – discover it!

God formed us, sin deformed us, but Christ reformed us. He redeemed us through His sacrifice for us, cleansed us from our faults and made us choice persons. He clothed us with a robe of righteousness and put upon us a crown of glory. What's more, God has chosen us to be for Him a royal priesthood, a holy nation, and a peculiar people. For this purpose, He has *....raised us up together, and made us to sit together in heavenly places in Christ Jesus.* (Eph. 2:6) That is our true position in Him.

It is God's desire for you to rise from the slum to the throne – to that position of biblical self-esteem. Picture yourself in this position of authority and power. See yourself walking in dominion, and hold these pictures in your mind continually. Remember, what you think you are, is what you will become! In other words, you are motivated to become what you imagine yourself to be. If you think healthy thoughts, happy thoughts, successful thoughts, and imagine yourself to be that, what you think about and give your attention to, reveals itself. Someone once said, "The difference between the successful man and the unsuccessful man is not so much a matter of training or equipment. It is just in the way that each of them looks at things."

You Are Valuable

Know that you are a person of worth. Your worth has very little to do with your possessions, salary, or position. Your biblically-based self-esteem has nothing to do with what you have or don't have. Recognise your worth, appreciate it, enjoy it, and keep reaffirming to yourself that you are a person of worth. You received all your worth and value when God gave you the gift of life. Be your best and live up to the value that was built in you at the beginning.

Base your opinion of yourself on internal standards and what God says about you, rather than on what others say. Give life your best. You are capable of reaching your potential. You can be more successful, more enthusiastic, and have a more fruitful life. You are valuable right now just being you; you are loved, respected, and appreciated by somebody right now – simply for who you are. You are capable of becoming great and holding a world title at something worthwhile; discover what it is.

The truth is, you have inbuilt inner value and because of that value, you can enjoy self-respect. You have tremendous inner worth, and if you are living up to that inner worth with integrity, which leads to self-respect, your potential is practically limitless. Whatever you have achieved in your life so far is the tip of the iceberg compared to what's possible for you. You can do more, be more, and have more in life.

Building positive self-esteem is the first step towards reaching all your potential. If you have any problem appreciating your self-worth, it is probably because there is one great truth you have yet to discover.

You Are Worth More Than Six Million Dollars

In his devotional book, *Alive*, S. Rickly Christian describes how one Yale University biochemist set out to quantify in dollar terms the infinite preciousness of human beings. He writes:

Working with a chemistry supply company's catalogue, Harold J. Morowitz began tabulating the exact value of the human body. Hemoglobin ran $285 a gram; insulin, $47.50 a gram; human DNA, $76; collagen, $15; and alkaline phosphate, $225, among others. On the more expensive side were such chemicals as bradykinin (amino acid), which sold for $12,000 per gram; follicle-stimulating hormone, $8 million a gram; and prolactin, the hormone that stimulates female milk production, $17.5 million per gram. When the price list was completed, Morowitz calculated how much of each chemical was in the human body and came up with an average value per gram of the human body at $245.54. Multiplying that amount by his dry weight (68 per cent of the body is water), he tallied his final value: $6,000,015.44.[1]

Wow! Have you ever sat down to think about your physical worth, not to talk of your infinite mental capacity? Even when you think you are down to zero, and when you think you are nothing and have nothing, at the very least, you are still worth more than $6,000,000.00! How many people would throw away a house, car, jewellery, or some other treasured possession worth $6,000,000.00? Yet how many people today neglect, misuse, abuse, or even engage in self-destructive activities and habits that degrade this precious gift of the human body!

After an objective self-analysis, S. Rickly Christian made the following confession, which, I believe, is true of the majority of people. Let's hear him:

My problem is that I'm generally not aware of my six million-dollar body...on a day-to-day basis, I'm more awestruck by the apparent miracle of architects and engineers who built the New York skyscrapers and Columbia Space Shuttle. When I look in the mirror each morning, I don't think, 'wow, God, thanks for splurging on my body!' instead I think 'if I could just get rid of the zit on my nose ...' and if God were to open the door for body alterations, I'd elbow my way to the front of the line.[1]

Another great truth you must always remember is that you are not inferior to anyone. An inferiority complex is only a state of mind – one with negative consequences. The people who succeeded in life and etched their names in the annals of greatness did so because they learnt how to utilise their God-given potentials, yielded themselves to God's purpose for their lives, and somehow learnt how to use most of His grace, power and abilities in them. Most of these people were created ordinary men, like you and me. But they learnt to do extraordinary things with what they were given. They, like all of us, were created in the image of God. God did not add one inch to His image in them, neither did He diminish by an inch His image in you when He created you. The difference, I believe, lies in the degree to which we yield to Him, and the extent to which the special grace and ability He has given to every man is put to use.

I believe God created every single individual to be great in his own way. If people are small, it is because they have not learnt how to achieve greatness, and have not discovered in what areas they can be great. Those who have discovered the secret have, like agitated electrons, broken away from the lower energy level of smallness and mediocrity to the higher energy level of success and greatness. Never make the mistake of putting yourself down. You too can be great, because you have the seed of greatness in you.

If men would only discover their real value and potential, they would spend less time lamenting their inadequacies.

In talking about the ignorance of men of themselves, S. Rickly Christian is not alone. Another apostle of the same school of thought is William Penn, the founder of Pennsylvania. On the subject of *Ignorance* in one of his writings published in the Harvard Classics, and titled *Fruits of Solitude*, William Penn made the following sobering and thought-provoking remark:

If one went to see Windsor Castle, or Hampton Court, it would be strange not to observe and remember the situation, the building, the gardens, fountains... that make up the beauty and pleasure of such a seat... And yet, few people know themselves; no, not their own bodies, the houses of their minds, the most curious structure of the world of which it was made, and out of which it is fed; which would be so much our benefit, as well as our pleasure, to know. We cannot doubt of this when we are told that the invisible things of God are brought to light by the things that are seen; and consequently we read our duty in them as often as we look upon them, to him that is the great and wise author of them, if we look as we should do.[2]

Learn To Use Your Endoscope Correctly

William Penn implied that there is much more to be discovered if we *"look as we should do."* Another philosopher, Lord Chesterfield, has suggested that you must look into people as well as at them. But how do we *"look into people,"* and by what means can *"looking as we should do"* be achieved? I guess what Lord Chesterfield has not told us is that people have potential – inbuilt talents and abilities – much more than meet the eyes. He should have told us that the true value of anything is internal, rather than external. I hasten therefore to say that looking into people suggests looking at them from the perspective of their own potential. More than that, it also suggests looking at people from God's point of view.

In looking as we should do, I do not think that we need a telescope (for we do not need to look too far), neither do we need to look through a microscope. But we do, however need a spiritual eye, one that I call the 'spiritual endoscope.' What I mean is that we need to look beyond that which is physically obvious.

I believe that when God created man, He also built into him a special ability to look inwards and see himself as God sees him, i.e. with all the innate gifts and talents built in him, some of which are not immediately apparent to the naked eye.

We are told in the book of Proverbs chapter 20 verse 27: *The spirit of man is the candle of the LORD searching all the inward parts of the belly.*

Every single individual has this special ability – what I like to call 'the inbuilt endoscope.' This 'endoscope' works in every one of us. If used properly (it can also be wrongly used), you will discover and steadily tap into the treasure reserve tucked away in you.

To a medical doctor, an endoscope is a device used to examine the interior of body cavities. It is used to view and discover what is on the inside rather than what is on the outside of a person. To you and me in this book, let's take this 'inbuilt endoscope' to mean a device by which we can look into ourselves and examine the spiritual and mental cavities to discover what gifts and abilities are in there. With this device, we can see what physical eyes cannot see; we can see – from the perspective of their potential – through, as well as into people. It is through this means that God stirs up in us the consciousness of the real self.

The majority of people have unfortunately not learnt to look at things from the positive side. Instead of looking inwards through this special device to discover the deposit of power and unique abilities in them given by God to help reach their maximum potential, all they see is the periphery, the trivial externalities – their physical, mental, and social handicaps and limitations. Hence, they develop an inferiority complex and failure consciousness that cripple their God-given abilities. This negative attitude and wrong approach to life is the string that has tied many potential achievers to the stake of mediocrity and kept them in a rut. Small wonder such individuals never achieve anything great in life in spite of their inbuilt potential; it is because their endoscope – the ability to look inwards and see themselves through God's eyes – is completely out of focus. Consequently, they are never able to see anything good in themselves. It is exactly the same way as a microscopist (one who uses a microscope) will never see anything sensible through his instrument until it is properly focused.

Those who do not recognise this ability in themselves are many. They go about looking elsewhere for what is already in them waiting to be appreciated. In consequence, they go through life groping in the darkness of unrealised dreams and crippled potential.

"What lies before us, and what lies behind us" says Ralph Waldo Emerson, "are tiny matters compared to what lies in us." How true is this statement by Emerson! God has placed within you all that you need to fulfil all that you were born to become and to do in life. You have within you the raw material for greatness. The real you is more than meets the eye. *Greater is he that is in you than he that is in the world.* (John 4:4*)*

I have given some thought to what Russell Stannard meant when he made the statement, "You are made of stardust."

If we unpack this statement by the British scientist to try to examine its content, I believe we will find in it the following meaning:

You are made of rare and expensive stuff, therefore,

You are precious.

You are valuable.

You are special.

You are unique, just the way God made you.

The following poem by Russell Kelfer tells you more about who you are:

You are who you are for a reason.
You're part of an intricate plan.

You're a precious and perfect unique design,
Called God's special woman or man.

You look like you look for a reason.
Our God made no mistake.
He knit you together within the womb,
You're just what he wanted to make.

The parents you had were the ones he chose,
And no matter how you may feel,
They were custom-designed with God's plan in mind,
And they bear the Master's seal.

No, that trauma you faced was not easy.
And God wept that it hurt you so;
But it was allowed to shape your heart
So that into his likeness you'd grow.

You are who you are for a reason,
You've been formed by the Master's rod.
You are who you are, beloved,
Because there is a God!

Russell Kelfer

Until you use your potential, you cannot add value to your generation. But how can you use potential that has not been developed? How can you develop potential that you have not yet discovered? And how can you begin the journey to discovery if you don't even as much as know you have potential? This book will help you with the answers to these key questions.

POINTS TO PONDER

- You are fearfully and wonderfully made to be unique and special in every way, made to fulfil a special plan in creation.
- What you think you are is what you are most likely to become. You are more than meets the eye, but you cannot be greater than the you that you know you are. You are motivated to become what you imagine yourself to be.
- You are valuable to God because you are worth more than $6,000,000.00.
- You have an inbuilt endoscope. Learn to use it correctly.
- The day you discover your purpose for living, that is the day you stop merely existing and start really living, whether you are 18 or 81.
- Until you use your potential, you cannot add value to your generation. But how can you use potential that has not been developed? How can you develop potential that you have not yet discovered? And how can you begin the journey to discovery if you don't even as much as know you have potential? This book will help you with the answers to these key questions.

> *There is radiance and glory in the darkness,*
> *could we but see, and to see we have only to look.*[3]
> Fra Giovanni

APPLICATION ACTIVITIES

1. Mention three things that you appreciate most about yourself.

    i.

    ii.

    iii.

2. For each of the next seven days, identify something positive about your life for which you can give thanks. Take time each day to give thanks for each one of them.

3. In what ways has this chapter helped to lift your spirit and improve the way you view yourself? Make a short list below:

    i.

    ii.

    iii.

    iv.

Chapter Two

YOU HAVE POTENTIAL

*Few men in their life time come anywhere near
exhausting the resources dwelling within them.
There are deep wells of strength that are never used.
Richard Byrd*

We all are capable of making our mark in life. We are all capable of achieving great things, climbing to great heights, reaching great accomplishments. But, too many people have had their potential blocked or locked up in the cage of ignorance of their real self and their real abilities. *Man know thyself* is an ancient admonition. The folly of ignorance in connection with self is epitomised in the unfortunate eaglet that lived and died without ever flying.

The Eagle That Never Flew

After laying her egg, mother eagle died. To incubate and hatch the egg, it was placed among chicken eggs in a chicken's nest.

As this young eaglet emerged from her egg, welcomed into the world by a gentle breeze and a stream of sunray that filtered into the bird's nest, she stepped into the world with several other chicks as siblings and mother chicken as benefactor. The eaglet grew up with the chickens, scratching the ground and pecking grains, insects, and worms like all the others. On the outside, she could tell that she was different from all the others, and deep down in her gut feeling, she could sense she was more than just a chicken. But as she grew up, she was programmed to behave like a chicken and to believe that she was no different from the rest of the chicks. She led a quiet, peaceful and successful life of ignorance – ignorance of her real self, real abilities, and real potential.

One day, as the chicks filed behind mother hen out in the field to forage for food, scratching and pecking as they went, the young eaglet looked up the sky and saw a mother eagle gliding and soaring overhead, high up in the sky.

"Oh! How I wish I could fly like that eagle!" exclaimed the ignorant eaglet.

"Don't be ridiculous," said one of the chickens. 'You are a chicken and nothing more, so don't even think about it."

To her own undoing, the eaglet accepted the wise counsel of a chicken and never attempted to fly. Thus, a strong, powerful 'leopard of the air' – as the eagle is known – lived among weak and feeble chickens the rest of her life, and never flew because she didn't know she had flight potential.

As long as she remained ignorant of her potential, the eaglet remained in the class of chickens and pecked at insects and grains like them. If she had discovered her true self, if she had recognised her potential, she would have known that she belonged to a bigger, better, higher class – the eagle class – and would have broken away from the lower class of chicken to the higher class, the eagle class, where even the sky is no longer the limit.

Many people today are like the ignorant eaglet. They are in the dark about their real powers, opportunities, abilities, and authority. It is the intention of this book to help you appreciate your real worth and find your path to freedom; to help you unlock your potential and put in your hands your passport to greatness. So, believe in yourself. You have the seed of greatness in you. You belong to the eagle class, not the chicken class. You too can soar high above mediocrity and self-imposed limitations, and become all that God wants you to be. You are wired for greatness, accept nothing less. Never allow anyone to talk you into a state of perpetual mental imprisonment. The time has come for you to grab your passport and take off to the land of freedom and greatness where you truly belong. The time is NOW to break away from the chicken mentality that has crippled and mummified your potential in the sarcophagus of mediocrity. There is an eagle in you waiting to soar. It is up to you to spread your wings and fly.

We will never know the number of geniuses who went to their graves unfulfilled, unknown, unrecognised, uncelebrated, simply because they didn't know what talents, and vast mental and spiritual capabilities they possessed.

Not everybody can be famous, but everybody can be great because greatness is a function of service, and service is the end result of potential. You have potential – latent powers, abilities, talents, and endowments capable of development into actuality. God gave them to you because He has a plan for your life, a special calling to do something for Him and for the world. That is called mission. To everyone He has given diverse talents, gifts, and special abilities to develop and put to use. Discover them. When you identify the area in which you have been called to serve, that becomes your mission. Your potential will define your mission, and your mission is tied to your potential. Your purpose on earth is to fulfil your mission. As your mission develops and becomes clearly defined, it becomes a ministry. So, your ministry is an outworking of your mission. Your present level of accomplishment is a direct result of the extent to which you have been able to discover, develop, and put to use this potential. Greatness is measured by service. The more people you serve with your gifts and talents, the greater you are likely to become.

In his epistle to the Colossians, Paul wrote in Chapter 4 verse 17: *And say to Archippus, take heed to the ministry which thou has received in the Lord, that thou fulfil it.*

Whenever God gives anyone an assignment, He always provides the necessary equipment and resources to accomplish the task. God never wastes anything, neither does He do or give anything without a reason. He did not give you interests, gifts, talents, and your personality as trophies to hang on your walls. They were given for a reason. He wants you to use your natural interests to serve Him and others. If you understand these facts, you can easily discover God's will for your life. Real joy and satisfaction come only by doing the will of God for your life and serving Him and others with the abilities He has given you.

The little child of today has growth potential. God has already put in him everything it takes for a normal child to grow and develop into a mature adult. So, the fact that a child is small today does not mean that he cannot be big tomorrow. Put him in the right environment, provide him with the nourishment his body needs, and give him a good education, and a proper spiritual, moral and social upbringing, and it will amaze you as you watch this child grow and develop physically, mentally, spiritually, morally, socially, and intellectually into a healthy, responsible, mature, and talented adult.

Apart from growth potential, a new-born child has other success potential that he must be helped to discover and develop as he grows.

"Give me a child," demands one psychologist, "and I will turn him into whatever you want him to be." This psychologist recognised the potential in a child, and that it is capable of development into anything. That is why children must be helped by parents and teachers to discover their potential early in life and begin to develop them.

The senile retiree who has lived all his life with nothing to show for it in terms of success and achievement lived so because he failed to discover and put to use his God-given potential. And someday, he will have to stand before his Creator and account for this waste of life and talent.

The Power Is Yours for the Asking

Don't give up! Don't just lie there defeated and frustrated! If you have fallen or failed once, rise up, dust yourself down, and go again. You can defeat defeat, master failure, turn your stumbling blocks into stepping stones, your frustration into fertiliser, and your downturns into dangling keys for success and achievement.

You have in your hands the power to get wealth. The scripture says, *And you shall remember the Lord your God, for it is He who gives you power to get wealth...* (Deuteronomy 8:18, NKJV)

If you are a child of God, then you have at your disposal the benefit of the grace of God, the power of the name of Jesus, and the treasure of the Word of God. That makes an indomitable combination.

Besides, the angels of God are on your side, the power of God's Holy Spirit is yours for the asking, and already, God has given you the power to make wealth. What more can you ask for!

You have the potential to live a successful and victorious life. How? *Because greater is he that is in you than he that is in the world. 'he that is in the world'* speaks of circumstances of life, antagonists, negative influences and individuals, sin, failure, frustrations, ignorance, disadvantaged background, poverty, etc.

You also have the potential to be great and successful in every area of your life. You can do the impossible, move your mountains, and capture your dreams. Paul affirmed, *I can do all things through Christ which strengthens me.* (Philippians 4:13)

Affirm it to yourself! You too can! In whatever area you want to activate your success potential, there is a common denominator – JESUS CHRIST. The moment Jesus steps into your life, your endoscope automatically swirls into the right focus; you begin to discover your real self; you become stuffed with power like a dynamite waiting to explode, and with the slightest spark, you go BAM!

A personal experience with Jesus Christ is indispensable in reaching your greatest potential. It is He who brings out the best in you and removes the worst. So then, the first step towards being all you can be is a personal knowledge of Jesus Christ and developing a close personal relationship with Him.

Now, do not dismiss this with a wave of the hand as some sort of senseless superstition. To develop a close relationship with Him is neither a weakness nor folly. On the contrary, it is wisdom and the very fountain of real power. And to be sure, this is not opinion, it is a fact tried, tested and proven from the dawn of time to be effective by millions of successful people all over the world.

I can hardly think of any other method that is as sure and as fail-proof as this one. Defeated men who encountered Him have rediscovered themselves and risen up in great victory; ask Abraham Lincoln. Quitters who gave Jesus a chance in their lives have staged heroic comebacks. Failures who called Him into their situations have stunned the world with stupendous success as they discovered Him and used their success potential. Lots and lots of suicidal people have forgotten their frustrations and decided to live, and really live, because they found in Him a reason to live. Shreds of shattered, battered, and broken marital relationships have been picked up, pieced together and made into a sweeter and better replica of the original thing because the name of Jesus was welcomed in. Derelicts who met with Him have been changed into decent people. Misguided souls who have found Him have been transformed into persons who possess the wisdom of the ages. I have seen these miracles happen right before my eyes, and they will happen again and again to those who believe in Him. So, making Jesus Christ your Senior Partner right now is not only one of the greatest and most important decisions you will ever make, it also automatically qualifies you to be recruited into an elite corps of achievers. This formula never fails. Try it!

The moment you develop a relationship with Christ, He gives you power to become... find out what in John 1:12.

With Jesus in you, and this mighty, crashing, explosive power, which can be summoned to your aid at will, you now have what I call MIGHTY POTENTIAL! You are now ready to defeat defeat, handle the impossible, turn stumbling blocks into stepping stones and capture your dreams; you become a mighty man or woman of valour; you are ready to dare any devil and take any bull by the horn!

Having reached this state, the next logical step that involves channelling this new-found power positively, creatively, and profitably in a manner that will benefit both you and the rest of humanity is to discover your place in God. By this is meant knowing what God has called you to be or do. Recognising your area of calling is a key element in reaching your maximum potential. The majority of people neglect this important aspect and pursue other people's dreams. Consequently, they end up defeated, frustrated, unaccomplished, and unfulfilled, in spite of their great potential.

Receiving and recognising how to use the powers God has offered to you, discovering your area of calling, and pursuing it vigorously with God's help are the secrets to unlocking your success potential. The scripture in 1 John 4:4 says, *Greater is he that is in you than he that is in the world.*

Two Men of Faith and Vision

Joshua and Caleb, two great warriors of ancient Israel, are men that were on time to discover the secret. That is why their faith stood unshakable in the most difficult test of their lives.

Joshua and Caleb were among twelve scouts that were assigned to go and spy out the land of Canaan and see what the land was like, and what the people who lived in the land were like. This story is contained in the book of Numbers chapter 13. This they did according to the instruction of the Lord through Moses. But ten of the scouts incited the people of Israel against Moses and Aaron on their return from this scouting expedition when they came back with a very negative report: *"We went to the land where you sent us. It truly flows with milk and honey, and this is the fruit."* (verse 27)

This was the first part of their report. Everything would have been just fine if only they stopped here. But no, not the ten spies! They continued, this time with a bad report: *"Nevertheless,"* said *they, "the people who dwell in the land are strong; the cities are fortified and very large; moreover we saw the descendants of Anak there."* (Verse 28)

This report brought fear and discouragement in the camp of Israel. Their report shows clearly that these men had quickly forgotten all the great acts of miraculous deliverance that God had performed in their midst right from their days in Egypt. In their unbelief, the 10 spies continued with their discouraging report in verse 31: *"We are not able to go up against the people, for they are stronger than we."*

But that's not all. It gets even worse in verse 32: *And they gave the children of Israel a bad report of the land which they had spied out, saying, "The land through which we had gone as spies is a land that devours its inhabitants, and all the people whom we saw in it are men of great stature.”*

As if that was not enough, the spies continued with their negative report in verse 33: *“There we saw the giants (the descendants of Anak came from the giants); and we were like grasshoppers in our own sight, and so we were in their sight.”*

That was the report of the ten spies. While these ten spies saw themselves as grasshoppers and chickened out from confronting their enemies because their faith was weak and their hearts melted in fear, Caleb and Joshua, the remaining two spies, stilled the people in verse 30, as Caleb reaffirmed in strong, unshakable faith: *“Let us go up at once and take possession, for we are well able to overcome it.”* (Numbers 13:30, NKJV)

Their faith saw them through. They went for it! They got it! These two spies have a record in history books as the only two adult Jewish survivors that made it to the promised land. Their faith and positive attitude saw them through.

Joshua and Caleb knew who they were in God. This knowledge of who a person is in God will always make unmovable movers, and bold, daring men out of cowards. Writing to Timothy in 2 Timothy 1:7, Paul said, *For God hath not given us the spirit of fear; but of power, and of love, and of a sound mind.*

As a kid, David son of Jesse discovered this secret when he was shepherding in the wilderness. Little surprise that he tore lions and bears in shreds and stepped out in faith demanding the head of Goliath, the Philistine Colossus, when even Saul, the King, and all his lieutenants fled at the defiant voice of the Philistine giant.

“Let no man’s heart fail because of him,” David encouraged, and with faith as unruffled as a concrete pillar in a gentle breeze, he adds, *“thy servant will go and fight with this Philistine”* (1 Samuel 17:32).

He went! He fought!! He conquered!!!

While Saul and his men saw Goliath as a giant too big to fight, David saw him as a target too big to miss.

The scripture again says: *But there is a spirit in man: and the inspiration of the Almighty giveth them understanding."* (Job 32:8)

There is, indeed, a spirit in man. It is the same spirit that receives inspired ideas from the Creator and communicates it to your mind. It is activated the moment Christ comes in, and is catalysed by the inspired word of God that dwells in you. The same spirit in you, when activated, stirs up the power of your potential at critical moments.

Zerubbabel, a man who stands with faith as strong as steel, operated in the same principle. No wonder God's angel spoke clearly to Zechariah concerning him: *This is God's message to Zerubbabel: "Not by might, nor by power, but by my spirit, says the Lord Almighty – you will succeed because of my Spirit, though you are few and weak'. Therefore no mountain, however high, can stand before him!"* (Zechariah 4:6-7a, The Book)

If God Says It, Believe It

Many people out there have been mentally crippled, have had their dreams killed, and their great plans choked by people with small minds and little vision who made them believe that they were attempting the impossible.

Impossibility exists only in the minds of those who have no desire to pay the price for success. If you believe it and work hard towards it, you can have it; if you don't, you can never soar. It is time to break away from the class of mediocres who have been sentenced to a substandard life as a result of their grasshopper mentality. Find your place among the eagle class and stay there. Never allow anyone to talk you into a state of perpetual mental encapsulation. Break away from all the mental limitations holding you back and soar with your goals. You can do all things through Christ who strengthens you. If God says it, believe it. If you do, you will do great things.

These People Shone With Potential

Once in a great while, the world witnesses the emergence of people with extraordinary abilities and enormous brainpower. People who make headline news and write their names in history books because they somehow learnt to discover and make the most of their God-given abilities, early in life.

Cardinal Guiseppe Mezzofanti (1774-1849), the chief keeper of the Vatican Library in Rome, was the world's greatest linguist. He could use 11 languages, translate 114 and 72 dialects besides, and speak 39 of the languages. He had an excellent brain capacity.

Escape expert R. O. Leossen of Iceland performed an amazing feat that beats the imagination. He was locked in a cell, his hands tied behind his back with handcuffs and chains that would take a force of 2,800 lbs to break. His feet were foot cuffed and chained too. Yet he was able to get loose and out of the cell through a 28-mm-thick, 9-inch-wide glass window in 5 hours 50 minutes. To achieve this feat, he had to break some of the cell's brickwork.

A few kids too are early to discover their enormous potential. Janet Aitchison of England was the youngest author to have a book published. She broke this record by writing her first book, *The Pirates Tale,* when she was only five and a half, and she was six and a half when it was published in 1969.

We have heard of kids younger than ten who were film directors and inventors, and others who could speak several foreign languages.

The highest I.Q. of modern times belongs to Kim Ung-Yong of South Korea who tested at 210 at the age of 4 years 8 months in 1967. He could speak 4 languages, compose poetry and solve problems by an integral calculus. Both of his parents were university professors.

Whiz Kid Graduates from College At 13

That was the headline of a report in an edition of *FAME Weekly*, a weekly magazine published in Lagos. The story is both exciting and challenging and is about a 13-year-old kid called Masoud Karkehabadi.

The 13-year-old's a medical whiz kid just like the teenage doctor character in the TV series. Not only does Masoud have an I.Q of 200-plus, he just graduated from the University of California at Irvine with a pre-med degree.

Now the boy wonder is headed off to medical school and expects to be a practicing neurosurgeon by 16. "God willing, my patients will accept me and disregard my age", says Masoud modestly. "They must realise that I have a very good brain to accomplish this by the time I'm 16."

That's putting it mildly. The youngster from Mission Viejo, California, has been on learning overdrive since he was a mere infant. At seven months, Masoud was speaking in full sentences. At 18 months, he could read. When he was two years old, he programmed the family computer. And at four he could translate books from English into the Iranian language, Farsi.

He got his high school diploma at age seven. At nine, he was tutoring college students in advanced anatomy. And incredibly, Masoud's been involved in major research for the past two years to find a cure for Parkinson's disease. "His intelligence has to be a one in a million thing", says Masoud's full-time governess, Jacqueline Holden. "And yet he never lords his abilities over others."

Masoud's father, Mahmoud – a former Iranian Air Force Pilot turned car salesman and his mom, Alejandra, knew they had a prodigy on their hands when their young son displayed a fantastic ability to learn on his own.

"At 18 months, he was reading highway signs from his car seat, telling his parents which exits to take," said Jacqueline. He learned to read with kids' books but quickly outgrew them. When he was two, Masoud picked up all the instruction booklets on how to programme the family home computer – and mastered it.

He learned Farsi, his parents' native tongue, at age four when his aunt came to America to study nursing. Little Masoud helped translate her English textbooks into Farsi so she could learn faster. Masoud's parents couldn't send him to public school because he was too smart. They had tutors instruct Masoud at home until he was seven but he didn't need them.

"I was absorbing so fast the tutors could not keep up with me," said Masoud. He mastered algebra, showed a passion for astronomy and especially loved to learn about anything medical. When he got his high school equivalence diploma at age seven, he scored 100 percent on the test. His folks then let him spend two years studying on his own and just being a boy, before they enrolled him in college at age nine. Older students teased Masoud at first but he solved that problem.

"What he did to make friends was help the other students in his upper division anatomy class," said Mahmoud. Masoud wound up tutoring 25 students who were struggling in anatomy and earned their total respect.

For the past two years at college, Masoud has been helping university professor Dr. Paul Fallon with research on Parkinson's disease. "Masoud's a genius without question," said Dr. Fallon. "He's doing things 20 to 25-year-old students have trouble getting a handle on."[4]

I am persuaded that the success potential, the ability to do what you are doing with skill and excellence, is inherent in every person with average intelligence. If this is true – and I firmly believe it is – why then do some people become top performers and others do not? Either early recognition of the presence of this innate potential, or ignorance of it, seem to be the most accurate responses to that question. Knowledge of a person's own potential makes him believe he can do things. He is motivated to be an achiever and becomes aware that he can overcome all adversities in the process. The dynamic power of his potential keeps him going, striving, thinking, believing, and forever trying through all the vicissitudes of his career.

The Call of Bezaleel and Aholiab

As the children of Israel set out for the promised land, two Jews, Bezaleel Uri and Aholiab Ahisamach, were called by God and He dished out a huge chunk of potential to perform a special task, namely, the building of God's sanctuary. That portion of scripture reads:

See, the Lord hath called by name Bezaleel ... and he hath filled him with the spirit of God, in wisdom, in understanding, and in knowledge, and in all manner of workmanship; ... And he hath put in his heart that he may teach, both he and Aholiab ... Them hath he filled with wisdom of heart, to work all manner of works ... (Exodus 35:30,31,34,35)

Their call was special because the important task at hand – a divine task – was equally special, and special tools were needed to get it done. Thus, both men were well equipped to this end, and in their days, they were unsurpassed as architects, interior designers, sculptors, skilled goldsmiths, silversmiths, and brasssmiths. Their genius was also expressed in stonecutting, woodcarving, fashion designing and embroidery, besides being divinely trained as instructors and teachers in these fields. These two men are an epitome of what I love to call MIGHTY POTENTIAL.

This chapter has, so far, endeavoured to show that we all have potential. This potential is diverse and varied and comes in different shades. It can be present in degrees. We may have more or less, depending upon the individual. It may be increased by use or destroyed by neglect. It is not a sovereign irresistible force, which comes upon us as a seizure from above, it is a gift from God, but one which must be recognised and cultivated if it is to realise the purpose for which it is given.

God gave to Bezaleel and Aholiab wisdom, knowledge and special skills to build for Him a tabernacle. They recognised these abilities and used them to the fullest to fulfil their destiny and purpose. But you don't need to wait till you hear a voice calling you up to some 'Mount Horeb' and telling you, amidst thunder and lightning, that you too have potential. Neither do you need to sit back and recline in an easy chair and fold your arms like some holiday maker by the beach, and wait till you fall into a trance where you see an Almighty hand reach down to you from the clouds with an extra something in a platter of gold, or split your skull in two, before you rise up and acknowledge to yourself that you have got what it takes to become all that God wants you to be.

One who exclaims, "But I am not gifted! I don't have anything special in me, so I can't make any impact!" is only admitting his inability to use his 'endoscope' as he should. There are no special people; there are only some who are more able than others, and more aware than others because they have mastered the skill of employing their 'endoscopes' for self-analysis and self-discovery.

It is better to try our abilities and learn to use them creatively than to wait and never do anything.

The Creator has given to everyone – you included – a liberal share of potential. Believe you have it, for that is the first thing to do. Read this book several times over and make sure you understand and apply every principle here conveyed, and before long, you will grow your potential.

I now end this chapter by giving you my modified rendition of an ancient Chinese saying:

He who knows not, and knows not that he knows not, but thinks he knows, is a fool. Avoid him.

He who knows not, but knows that he knows not, and is willing to know what he knows not, is a student. Teach him.

He who knows, and knows not that he knows, and walks around thinking he knows not, is asleep. Wake him.

But he who knows, and knows that he knows, and knows how to use what he knows to the best of his knowledge, is a wise leader. Follow him.

If you always make it a point to know what you do know, know what you don't know, and know what you should know, you will always stay ahead of the pack.

- You belong to the eagle class not the chicken class. You too can soar high above poverty, ignorance and mediocrity.

- Your present level of accomplishment is a direct result of the extent to which you have been able to discover, develop, and put your potentials to use.

- You can defeat defeat, master your failures, turn your stumbling blocks into stepping stones, your frustration into fertiliser, and your downturns into dangling keys for success and achievement.

- The first step towards being all you can be, is to develop a personal relationship with Jesus Christ. It is He that brings out the best in you and takes out the worst.

- You can do all things through Christ who strengthens you. If God says it, believe it. If you do, you will do great things.

- Impossibility exists only in the minds of those who have no desire to pay the price for success. If you believe it and work hard towards it, you can have it; if you don't, you can never soar.

- There are no special people; there are only some who are more aware and more able than others because they have mastered the skill of employing their 'endoscope' for self-analysis and self-discovery.

- You are wired for greatness. Accept nothing less. There is an eagle in you waiting to soar. It is up to you to open your wings and fly

> *It is our failure to understand ourselves*
> *which causes most of our sufferings.*
> Dorothy Rowe

APPLICATION ACTIVITIES

1. What would you consider your greatest assignment(s) in life?

   i.

   ii.

   iii.

2. What can you do to scale that up to a global level so as to serve the maximum number of people?

3. If you do not have the answers to the above questions now, then proceed to chapter three. But I strongly advise you to come back to these questions after completing chapter three.

Chapter Three

DISCOVER YOUR POTENTIAL

There is something that is much more scarce, something far finer, something rarer than ability. It is ability to recognise ability.
Anonymous

In the last chapter, a deliberate attempt was made at consolidating and buttressing the fact that everyone, including you, has potential.

Agreed? Agree you should because the acceptance of this fact is not only a plus to your self-esteem, it forms the basis of the subject for consideration in this chapter.

It is one thing to know you have potentials – at least many people have a mental assent – but it is quite another to discover what potentials they are, and use them to advantage. It is not just enough to have a mental assent that you possess something; it is often wiser to go a step further and discover what it is.

One of our great sins, which we seldom even notice, is taking too much for granted. We tend to complain about little things, especially things we seem not to have, and fail to recognise and appreciate what we already have. We are surrounded by people who have latent and undeveloped traits that, through lack of self-analysis and consequent lack of self-knowledge, may long remain undiscovered or underutilised.

The Council of Wisdom

The following story is one that has intrigued me so much. It is a story that I have sat down to ponder deeply, and I believe that you too will find it as intriguing as I did and will learn a thing or two from it.

In this story, the King of Wisdom called his councillors together in a closed-door meeting to deliberate on a very important subject – the best and safest place to hide wisdom. Wisdom must be hidden such that only the right men who really search, and search the right way would find it. *I love those who love me, says the King of Wisdom, and those who seek me early and diligently shall find me.* (Proverbs 8:17, Amp). One of the councillors raised his hand to speak.

"I've got a fantastic idea," he said. "Let us hide wisdom on the top of the tallest mountain. Man will never find it there."

"Yea! That's a great idea!" everyone seemed to agree as they all roared in applause.

"No, my sons!" said the King of Wisdom as he motioned them to silence with a swift wave of His right hand. "I do not think this is a good idea," he cautions. "Man is a very adventurous creature. One day he will venture up the mountains, and there he will find wisdom. That's too easy."

There was silence for a moment as a gentle, quiet wave of nodding of heads swept through every section of the room – a sure indication that everyone agreed with the King of Wisdom. After a short while, another councillor got up to speak.

"In that case I suggest we hide wisdom deep inside the earth. Man will never find it there."

Again, the King of Wisdom was hesitant to agree.

"My son, man has an insatiable quest for knowledge" he pointed out. "One day he will devise a means to explore, excavate and mine the earth. Then he will invent a machine to help him drill deep down into the earth. Finally, one day, he will drill his way into the reservoir of wisdom."

Again there was silence for a moment as each councillor looked at the next one as if trying to find the missing piece of a puzzle from the look on his face. Then, suddenly, after a long deep breathe, another impatient councillor, breaking through the silence, announced:

"I have another wonderful idea," said this councillor, jumping to his feet and raising his hand at the same time. "Let's take wisdom into the bottom of the sea and hide it there. I'm certain that man will never find it there."

Everyone clapped and cheered, believing that this time they've got it. After the cheering and clapping had subsided, the King of Wisdom spoke once again.

"That was a brilliant attempt, my son. But you must also remember that we have given to man an immense creative ability. I am certain that one day he will put this to use and come up with an invention that will help him breathe under water. Then he will swim like a fish to the bottom of the sea, and there he will find wisdom."

At this reply from the King of Wisdom, all the councillors, now obviously out of ideas, sagged on their seats, heaving a sigh of despair.

There was silence. You could hear a pin drop.

Suddenly, yet another anxious councillor, leaping from his seat with a shout of excitement, and throwing his fist up in the air exclaimed:

"Yahoooo! I've got it!!" he exclaims. "This is what we've been waiting for. I suggest we take wisdom to outer space. There it will be hidden far away from the reach of man. I am certain, very certain this time that man will never find it there."

This ingenious suggestion from this clever councillor was greeted with wild excitement all over the meeting room as all the other councillors leaped to their feet, greeted one another with hi-fives and carried this brilliant councillor shoulder high for this fantastic idea. They have finally unravelled the puzzle, they thought to themselves, almost forgetting that this 'big idea' needed ratification from the King of Wisdom.

As the wild excitement continued, the King of Wisdom motioned for silence.

Another spell of dead silence was cast over the meeting room.

Every eye was now burning a hole in the face of the King of Wisdom as the councillors focused on him with rapt attention, sitting upright on the edge of their seats and waiting for what he had to say. The uneasy calm was becoming unbearable…hearts were beating faster and faster as the face of each councillor was now reflecting what looked like a chemical mixture of positive excitement, resignation and melancholia. Finally, after what seemed like ages, he spoke.

"Nice try my son," said the King of Wisdom, as his long awaited voice cut through the thick silence. "But you appear to have forgotten so soon the insatiable curiosity in man as well as his creative ingenuity," he continued. "I have no doubts at all that one day man will invent a flying machine that can take him anywhere through space, and out of his insatiable curiosity he will be tempted to explore outer space. And there, there my sons, he will discover the hidden place of wisdom."

"That's it," exclaimed one councillor. "I give up," he continued as he sank into his seat in utter surrender.

"We will never unravel this mystery," said another disappointed councillor, "never ever!" he gave in as he took his gaze off the King of Wisdom.

All the other councillors sat back, confused. They had exhausted their ideas. Their trump cards had all failed. It was useless trying again. All eyes were now focused on the King of Wisdom himself to provide the key to unravelling this mystery, the essential part to this complex jig-saw puzzle.

"What then shall we do to hide wisdom from man?" the councillors wondered. Their brains had been tasked, their wisdom tested, and their imagination has been stretched to the limit. Yet there appeared to be no satisfactory solution to this complex puzzle.

After this long and challenging session, the King of Wisdom finally overruled, and the council of wisdom rose from the meeting with one resolution:

Wisdom should be hidden, not on top of the tallest mountain, or buried under the earth, or hidden at the bottom of the sea. No, not even in outer space… but in the most unlikely place – inside man.

The True Source of Wisdom

True wisdom is inspired from above and revealed or generated from within in those who have learnt to walk with God – the Father, Giver and King of Wisdom.

An ungodly and unbelieving man will perpetually walk in folly and ignorance, though he be 'educated' or 'clever', because the wisdom of this world is foolishness with God (1 Cor. 3:19).

We are told in the book of Proverbs chapter 9 verse 10:

The reverent and worshipful fear of the Lord is the beginning (the chief and choice part) of Wisdom, and the knowledge of the Holy One is insight and understanding.

When you become a child of God and walk in the fear of the Lord, you become connected to the fountain of wisdom that God has hidden in you. You begin to draw from it. You have within you that wisdom potential waiting to be tapped into. As the fear of the Lord in your life deepens, His fountain of wisdom also grows and deepens in your life so that you are able to have deep insight and understanding. When you cease to fear the Lord, His wisdom in your life depletes.

Acres of Diamond

The title above is probably familiar to you if you have heard about a preacher called Russell Conwell. He is famous for a sermon which he preached many years ago and gave it the above title.

His sermon is all about a poor Boer farmer who owned a farm, but didn't know what to do with it. This was a man who was obsessed with the desire to be rich, owned a farm, but never knew the true value of his farm. Unknown to this farmer, this farm had the answer to all he was looking for. But in his ignorance, he struggled for many years to glean a livelihood out of his rocky soil, until finally, in despair, he sold the farm to another man and went off to seek his fortune elsewhere.

In the meantime, the new owner of the farm was out by the creek one day when he made a startling discovery. He happened to look down just as the sun caught something sparkling on the ground.

When he came closer to see what it was and picked it up, what did he see? He discovered, to his greatest amazement, that it was a costly piece of diamond. That one diamond later turned out to be one of the most precious diamonds ever discovered.

And the farm?

That same farm which, to the former owner, was barren and useless because in his ignorance he failed to discover its true value, became the world's most famous diamond mine.

And the poor Boer farmer?

When he came back to his old farm years later – still poor of course, he found it swarming with machinery and life – more wealth being dug out of it every day than he had ever dreamed existed. That mine was the great Kimberly Diamond Mine!

All around us are people no better than that poor Boer farmer. I say so because few people take time to discover the true value of what they have. They spend time so lamenting what they do not have that they are oblivious of all the blessings and goodness that God has bestowed upon their lives. So they are busy searching in faraway places for something that may just be right there with them waiting to be discovered and tapped into.

Such is the story of the poor Boer farmer. As the famous Nigerian saying goes: *What you are looking for in **Sokoto** (an ancient city in northern Nigeria) may well be right there under your **sokoto** (the Yoruba word for trouser in western Nigeria)*. Discover it.

Most people pass through life wandering around aimlessly without capturing their place and purpose in life. This is often because of ignorance, impatience, and a wrong – and often skin-deep – appraisal of their real worth and value. They struggle along under their surface power, never drawing from the giant power that could be theirs if they would but dig a little deeper and rouse their God-given potential that can give them even more than any acre of diamonds. This can be attributed to the wrong use of what I like to call the built-in 'Spiritual Endoscope'. People who have written themselves off as barren, unproductive, of no use, insignificant, and incapable, and given up on life without realising that their gold mine may just be one inspired idea from God bubbling from within them, are not a few.

There is no treasure in life that is not hidden. From pure natural spring water to crude oil, and from tin to gold, they are all hidden deep in the earth. They do not always come to the surface to be discovered by just anyone. It often takes diligent search to discover the vein of gold.

The deep treasures of the gift of scientific discoveries are uncovered only by research, by those who have devoted their lives and time to do so.

Your riches are hidden and waiting to be discovered. Search diligently and you will find them. But in searching, do not grope blindly in the dark. God gave them to you and put them in you. So go back to Him to show you where they are and how you can start digging. You will be amazed at what you will discover.

Whose Dream Are You Pursuing?

I have met lots and lots of people who pass through life with no dream of their own. They are simply busy pursuing other people's dreams. Back in my school day when I was in the A' Level class, many of the students in the science class wanted to study medicine. There is absolutely nothing wrong with that. The only problem was that most of them were under pressure from their parents who wanted to do anything to make sure their kids became doctors, whether they liked it or not. They were not allowed to have a say in the matter. Other students had friends who wanted to become doctors. So, they thought it was cool to follow suit and pursue the same dreams. They simply had no dream of their own.

"Your great grandfather was a doctor," said one mother to her son, "and your grandfather was also a doctor. Your father worked hard to become a doctor, so a doctor you must also be or you are no longer our son."

Henry, a good friend of mine, was one of such people. He was not allowed to have a life of his own. His mum was a nurse, so she was determined that her son became a doctor. So, on and on he struggled for many years to do what his mum wanted. He tried many times and wrote many exams to get into medical school, but things refused to work out.   Each trial only ended up in failure and frustration because he simply was not gifted in that area. For about six years, he kept on trying the university matriculation exam, putting medicine as his course of first choice. After wasting six full years of fruitless attempts, he decided to forget his mum's dreams and get a life of his own. He sat down one day, took inventory of his life and decided to be realistic and do what he really wanted. He decided to study law, which is where he felt his interest really was. He took the university matriculation exams again, this time with law as his first choice. He passed without much struggle and went on to study Law at the university.

I met Henry again during his second year in law school and asked him what it felt like changing his career goal from medicine to law. He said to me, "All these years, I've been busy pursuing my mum's dream and have been unsuccessful. But now I want to get real and pursue my own dream in life." He did and finally succeeded without any hassles. When I spoke to Henry again recently, he was doing very well, living the American dream in the state of Indiana as a practicing attorney.

For Henry, the sudden transition from medicine to law was seriously criticised by his mother and many close friends who thought that that was the craziest thing to do. But Henry did not allow all that to bother or discourage him. Today, Henry is a successful lawyer. With his extraordinary talent in music that he has greatly developed and is putting to use, and many other natural gifts and talents that he is still uncovering, Henry has finally found his path to greatness. Don't be content living with the results of other people's thinking. Live your dream. You've got to have a dream – your own dream – and keep it alive. When you lose your dream, you die. So don't stop dreaming. If you stop dreaming, you stop growing. If you stop growing, you start aging. And if you start aging, eventually you die.

There are so many people walking around who are dead and don't even know it.

So I ask you, whose dream have you been chasing? Your parents', your friends', or yours? Think about it! Never let the noise of other people's opinions and wishes drown out your own inner voice and passion. Life is like a very personalised assignment given to each one of us. Most people fail in life's assignment because they try to copy others, not realizing that everyone has been given a different assignment sheet. Others fail, not because they have not worked hard enough in life, but because they have been very busy working on the wrong assignment.

I recall a most fitting analogy about a college student who needed to complete an important assignment in order to graduate. After spending sleepless nights of study and many long hours in the library working on this major assignment, it was finally complete. He turned in the assignment and went home to wait for the result. When he received his paper back a few days later, he found that the professor had written the following words on the paper: "Good research. Great illustrations. Wonderful bibliography. Grade 'F.' – WRONG ASSIGNMENT."

There can be nothing as regrettable as acing the wrong assignment in life; nothing as painful as winning the wrong race, and nothing as disappointing as fulfilling someone else's destiny.

Goethe, the German philosopher, once said: *I augur better of a youth who is wandering on his own path than of many who are wandering aright on paths that are not theirs.*

Take his advice. Don't waste your time wandering in paths where you are not gifted. Don't waste your time running after another person's dream. Get a life of your own. Find your God-given dream and live it. Do not wander into territories where you know you do not belong. Find the path where you were meant to walk and stay there. That is the way to fulfil your purpose in life. Any other way will lead you down the road to an unfruitful life of unnecessary struggles, failure, and frustration. Believe me!

George Frederick Handel

Handel was an outstanding German composer who discovered his musical talents before he was 12. As a boy he was intensely interested in music, but his father was determined that he become a lawyer. Handel knew he was born to be a composer, not a lawyer. His musical genius had already become apparent and he played at the court of the King of Prussia when he was only twelve. So, Handel went on to study law at Halle University, handed the certificate to his father, and dashed off to continue with his first love, music, from where he left off. Handel became one of the leading figures in music and composed numerous operas and oratorios, including the immortal *Messiah*. Even blindness during the last seven years of his life did not discourage him from composing. Handel's greatest oratorio, the *Messiah*, for which he is best known, was first performed in 1742 in Dublin, Ireland, with Handel himself conducting. He had been commissioned to write an oratorio for a benefit program of the Dublin Foundling Hospital, and had composed this crowning masterpiece in less than twenty-five days. The first London performance occurred the following year. As the singers began the stirring 'Hallelujah Chorus', King George II of England was so inspired that he rose to his feet. The audience, too, stood up and remained standing until the chorus ended. George's action established a custom that is still followed till this day at many performances of the *Messiah*.

There Was an Engineer in Him

A man named Randall Hamrick was a renowned professional counsellor. He once met a young truck driver who needed help with the choice of a career because he was tired of his old job of truck driving.

During counselling, Randall Hamrick advised the truck driver, who was 25 years old at the time, to take a series of tests. After these tests, it was discovered that this young truck driver had such abilities that would put him at the top of the class in any engineering school. Just to be sure, the tests were repeated six times, and the results were the same. Hamrick then advised this young truck driver to go to an engineering school where his talents would be developed and creatively used.

The young truck driver was very reluctant at first because he did not believe that he really had what it takes. But after much persuasion from Hamrick, he decided he had nothing to lose. He went to school to give it a try.

A few years later, this truck driver graduated from the university with honours as the best student, and he became an outstanding engineer.

Sometimes one's potentials are very loud and obvious, but other times, it takes someone else to help one find them. The truck driver needed a push from Hamrick to bring his full potential to the fore. You can never fulfil your purpose in life if you do not discover your gifts and talents. Greatness in life and calling will elude you as long as your true potential remains buried. Your purpose in life is often revealed in your gifts and talents.

Your Natural Gifts Are the Keys to Discovering Your Pathway to Greatness

Johnson O'Connor and his foundation developed a method of testing individuals for their natural gifts and talents. The Johnson O'Connor Foundation carries out a battery of tests, which measure natural gifts in nineteen different areas. Following these tests, evidence has emerged that few people tested by Johnson O'Connor have more than seven aptitudes and usually the number is three to five.

To give you an idea of each test and the gift it identifies, here is a brief description:

Graphoria identifies clerical ability in dealing with figures and symbols. The test measures the ability to handle paperwork at high levels of speed and efficiency. Graphoria is necessary for bookkeeping, editing, secretarial tasks, and so on. It is also a real indicator of how well a person will do in school, where many subjects require this ability.

Ideaphoria indicates creative imagination of expression of ideas. It is extremely useful in fields such as sales, advertising, teaching, public relations, and journalism.

Structural visualisation tests the ability to visualize solids and think in three dimensions. It is an aptitude possessed by concrete thinkers who don't do as well with abstract thinking. It is an absolutely critical skill for engineers, mechanics, and architects.

Inductive reasoning helps an individual form a logical conclusion from fragmented facts. This ability is important for lawyers, researchers, diagnostic physicians, writers, and critics – all of whom must be able to move quickly from the particular to the general pattern and see the big picture from all the details.

Analytical reasoning is useful for writers, editors, and computer programmers who need to organise concepts and ideas into sequences or classifications.

These are just a few of the tests done in the Johnson O'Connor Foundation as given by Margaret E. Broadley in her book *Your Natural Gifts*.[5] This kind of testing is useful for helping people who wish to make career transitions or changes. People may also be helped to know why they may be frustrated and unhappy because of being in the wrong kind of work. Since most kids grow up with only a vague idea of what they really want to become in life, parents can help them early in life to take tests that will help reveal their natural gifts and talents. That would help introduce them to experiences that would provide the opportunity to develop their natural gifts and talents. If that can be achieved, it would provide a tremendous boost towards developing their lives along the path of greatest potential.

How to Discover Your Purpose and Potential

1.   Study the Owner's Manual

The easiest way to discover the purpose and capacity of an invention or product is to ask the creator of it. Every product or invention has a purpose. To fulfil that purpose, the creator usually builds into it all the required ability and capacity to reach its full potential and perform optimally.

To understand the full potential of an invention, its purpose, specifications, correct usage, care and maintenance tips, the manufacturer usually provides a user manual containing all the required details. If the user does not take time to carefully study this manual, the product could be misused, its potential could be underutilised, or the life span of the product could even be shortened because the manufacturer's instructions have not been carefully followed.

The same is true for discovering your full potential. You are God's special invention. He created you for a purpose and gave you a mission to fulfil on earth. To achieve that purpose and fulfil your mission on earth, He has built into you all the gifts, talents and abilities you require. Some are obvious, while others are not. God specially crafted and prescribed every single detail of your body. He selected for you your gender, race, colour of skin, and every other detail. He also determined the natural talents you would possess, and the uniqueness of your personality. Everything you need to fulfil your purpose in life has been provided. God left nothing to chance. So, to discover your purpose, your abilities, and every single detail about your life, you must turn to God – the owner, designer and creator of your life. You cannot discover God's purpose for your life by your own effort, but only through building a relationship with Him and seeking His guidance. He has not left us to wander in the dark and guess. He has provided for us an Owner's Manual – the Bible. In it He has explained our purpose, why we are alive, how we were made, what frame we were made from, how life works, our abilities, what to do, what not to do, and how to care for our lives and live longer. In this book is distilled the wisdom of the ages. Not only that, God has given us His Spirit to lead us into all truth. Talk to Him, read the manual, and ask His Holy Spirit to show you what and where all your potential has been stored. Contained in this Owner's Manual is a passage which states:

But it was to us that God made known his secret by means of his Spirit. The Spirit searches everything, even the hidden depths of God's purposes. It is only our own spirit within us that knows all about us... (1 Corinthians 2:10, 11a GNT).

God reveals the hidden depths of His purposes to us by His Spirit. So, as long as you stay connected to Him, your spirit will begin to pick up His purposes for your life and express them through your gifts, your passion, and the deep longings of your heart to pursue certain interests that are aligned to the purpose He has for you. Trust Him to lead and guide you. Many people today do not live long enough to fulfil their purpose, or are living substandard lives of ignorance, fear, insecurity, failure, lack of purpose, underachievement, physical and spiritual bondage, frustration, broken relationships – the list goes on – because they have either not taken time to carefully study this *owner's manual*, or have chosen to live in deliberate violation of the clear instructions contained in it.

2.   *Follow your heart*

The term *heart* is used severally to describe your desires, interests, dreams, ambitions and passions. Motivation comes from within – from the heart. You are motivated to do what you care about and what you love to do most. God has given to each one of us a heart for something – something we love to do or are passionate about, and possess the ability to do effectively. Listen to your inner promptings.

What are the things you care about the most? What are those things that you are interested in and love to do no matter how difficult they seem? Those are clues and pointers to where your pathway to greatness rests. When you are doing what you love to do, when you are doing what you are wired to do, you feel good inside, you feel a sense of satisfaction and fulfilment, and you need no one to motivate you or check up on you.

Are you passionate about certain interests, school subjects, topics, sports, skills, or areas of calling? Those inborn interests come from God. He gave you an emotional heartbeat for those interests. Don't ignore them. There is a reason you love those things. Your gifts and talents are often locked up in your interests. The more you pursue those interests, the more you unlock your gifts and talents, and the more you find fulfilment in doing so. But when you pursue what you are not wired to do, the result is much struggle, stress, waste of time and talent, lack of interest, failure, frustration, and discouragement. Be courageous enough to follow your heart and intuition. They somehow already know what you were meant to become.

3.   *Take a test*

Some professional counsellors and educational psychologists have devised ways and methods of testing people to help them discover their natural gifts and talents. These tests could be very useful in helping young people in the choice of career because they know from an early age where their strengths lie, what their natural abilities are, and what interests to pursue that are consistent with their natural abilities and talents. Consulting professionals, reading good books, taking tests, and doing simple exercises that help bring out the best in you and motivate you along the path of healthy, biblical self-evaluation and self-discovery are all a plus in your effort to discover your potential and path to greatness.

4.   *Take an inventory of your gifts and talents*

Take a long honest look at your entire life. What are you good at, and what are your limitations? Nobody is good at everything, and no one has been called to be everything. But, surely you are gifted and called to be and do something. Try to find out what it is, and don't let another day go by without doing just that. Apart from the Creator, you are the person who knows yourself the best. Where have you displayed abilities and gifts that other people have confirmed? Where are you having the most success in what you do? Do you have the talent to sing, to compose a song or write poetry, to play a musical instrument, or to draw and paint? Are you good in teaching, motivating young people, organising, or winning people over? Do you excel in acting, making people laugh and keeping them happy, or are you passionate about championing the course of justice, defending helpless victims of abuse and injustice, or leading people? Identify your strengths, abilities, inclinations, gifts and natural talents. Make a list of all that you are able to identify. Display the list in a place where you can see and read it every day, for in that list is contained your key to greatness. Concentrate on developing them further and putting them to use. You will generally excel and be effective when you do what God has gifted you to do.

5.   *Ask those who know you well.*

Sometimes we are oblivious of what we have, or take them for granted. As part of your gifts and talents inventory, you should ask close friends and relatives who know you well for some help in discovering your potential. Let them know you are searching for the truth and not compliments of some sort, and ask them to help you search for the truth about yourself and the gifts, talents, and positive inclinations they have noticed in you. It certainly helps to get feedback from those who know you best. Let them tell you what they think you are good at doing and what you're not good at. If you think you are good at doing something and no one seems to agree, then think again.

6.   *Start using your known gifts.*

When you discover your abilities and use them in a manner consistent with the plan of God for your life, you experience satisfaction, fulfilment, and a new surge of energy. In the process, you discover more gifts and talents that you never knew were there.

God expects you to start using your talents; make the most of them and stop worrying too much about the ones you don't have or have not yet discovered. Start using your gifts and talents in new and exciting ways. Try doing things you haven't done before. It is in doing so that you discover the dozens of hidden abilities and gifts you've got. Your life is loaded with unopened gifts. You will never know all that's in you till you start opening those gifts. Get involved in a new sport, experiment with writing poetry and songs, try your hand at a new musical instrument, keep on experimenting and keep on discovering. You will never really know all that you are gifted at unless you try. Never say "I can't." That is the alibi of the mediocre. If you try something and it doesn't work out, see it as an experiment, not a failure.

A boy was sitting in class playing with his tie instead of paying attention to his teacher. The teacher caught him and decided to punish him for his lack of attentiveness. As punishment, he was asked to stand in front of the class and sing a song. He had never sung before, so he was confused at first, not knowing what to sing. But he decided to make up his own song right there and then and sing it his own way. That was exactly what he did. At the end of his singing, it became clear to everyone that this boy was gifted as an opera singer. That was how he discovered his gift of singing. Presently, this 15-year-old boy has enrolled in a school where he is receiving some training to develop his gift in classical music as he aspires to become a professional artist. You will never know what you are capable of doing till you start doing things. It doesn't matter whether you are 15 or 50. It's never too late. Perhaps you have heard the story of a frail mother who lifted up a whole automobile to save her son stuck under it. It is just one example of the tremendous latent powers locked up in us waiting for the right moment to be released.

> *Surround yourself with the dreamers and the doers, the believers and thinkers, but most of all, surround yourself with those who see greatness within you, even when you don't see it yourself.*
> Anonymous

POINTS TO PONDER

- As the fear of the Lord in your life deepens, His fountain of wisdom also grows and deepens in your life so that you are able to have deep insight and understanding. When you cease to fear the Lord, His wisdom in your life depletes.

- What you are looking for in **Sokoto** may well be right there under your **sokoto.**

- There can be nothing as regrettable as acing the wrong assignment in life; nothing as painful as winning the wrong race, and nothing as disappointing as fulfilling someone else's destiny.

- Don't waste your time wandering in paths where you are not gifted. Don't waste your time running after another person's dream. Find your God-given dream and live it. Find the path where you were meant to walk and stay there.

- Your purpose in life is often revealed in your gifts and talents.

- The more you pursue your interests, the more you unlock your gifts and talents and find fulfilment in doing so. When you pursue what you are not wired to do, the result is much struggle, stress, waste of time and talent, lack of interest failure, frustration, and discouragement.

- Your life is loaded with unopened gifts. You will never know all that's in you till you start opening those gifts.

- If you try something and it doesn't work out, see it as an experiment, not a failure.

> *I submit to you that if a man hasn't discovered something that he will die for, he is not fit to live.*
> Martin Luther King, Jr.

1. What gifts and talents have you discovered already in yourself? Make a list of them below.
   a.
   b.
   c.
   d.
   e.

2. Ask your closest friends what gifts and talents they think you have. Make a second list below.
   a.
   b.
   c.
   d.
   e.

3. Compare the items on list 1 and 2 above. Take note of the items that correspond. Those are areas where you are obviously gifted.
   a.
   b.
   c.

4. Make a third list below of those items in (1) and (2) above that correspond.
   a.
   b.
   c.

Chapter Four

DEVELOP YOUR POTENTIAL

Talent is like a picture taken by a camera.
To amount to anything, it needs developing.
Frank Tyger

We all have great potential. God gave each one of us the potential for spiritual, physical, emotional, mental, and intellectual growth and development. Most people have not fully exploited their potential. Others have managed to discover some of their potential, but have done little or nothing to develop it. A few others have developed one aspect of their potential and that's all. They have experienced growth and success in that one area only, and have sat down in the chair of complacency telling themselves they have now arrived. What about the rest? I know of great sportsmen and women who discovered their sporting talents, developed them, and somehow managed to use them to achieve stardom. Then they sat down and did nothing more. What about their mental and intellectual capabilities? Those are left neglected, uncultivated, and allowed to rot. Apart from their sporting potential, every other gift and talent that God gave to them is abandoned in the gutter to die – like some unwanted baby that was delivered by a school-going teenager at the wrong time.

Every tree has branches, and each branch receives supplies and nourishment from the roots. When the branches are nourished and nurtured, they develop, blossom, and produce healthy flowers and fruits. If a branch fails to receive nourishment from the roots for any reason, that branch simply dies off, and it dies with all its potential – the numerous flowers, fruits and seeds it would have produced.

You are like the tree. Each branch on the tree represents the various outlets through which your potential can be unleashed when developed. Some people have been able to develop most of their potential. That is why they are said to be multi-talented. Every branch of your God-given potential is gasping for life. You need to nourish and nurture as many of these branches as you can, till they each grow to full potential and blossom like flowers, and till you begin to radiate the power of your full potential.

Celebrated sportsmen and women excelled in their fields of endeavour because they recognised their sporting potential, trained long and hard at developing them, and grabbed the opportunities that came along to put them to use. Renowned writers and poets recognised that they had these abilities in them. They dug them up, refined them, and used these abilities to achieve for themselves world recognition. Great men of God were so recognised because they developed their spiritual gifts and talents, placed them at the service of the Lord, and became instruments of healing and transformation to thousands of people whose lives they have touched.

If you develop your intellectual potential, you become a great intellectual; if you develop your sporting potential, you become a great sportsperson; if you develop your acting and musical gifts and talents, you become a great name in show business. It is that simple.

> *Some people have a hundred acres of possibilities*
> *and about half an acre is under-cultivated.*
> Unknown

Refuse to be counted among people with very good brains and extremely creative minds who are living a wasted life in the slums of mediocrity because they failed to use their creative minds creatively and profitably.

Butterfly or Caterpillar?
If you have ever been a biology student, then you are probably familiar with the different metamorphic changes that occur during the

life cycle of a butterfly. It all begins with the laying of eggs by the adult butterfly, which then hatches into a worm-like larva known as a caterpillar. The active worm-like caterpillar resembles anything but a butterfly. It is an eating machine that ravages anything green and leafy across its path as it wiggles through crops and vegetation. I suppose it must have earned itself the name 'caterpillar' because of its destructive nature.

After the larva stage, this creature metamorphoses into the next stage, an inactive pupa stage, after spinning a cocoon around itself. The pupa usually clings onto a twig and remains in this cocooned state for some days. During this time some internal physiological changes take place within the cocoon. The bodily features of the adult butterfly begin to develop and take shape. These changes continue within the cocoon or puparium for about one to two weeks, until finally, a colourful, beautiful, fully developed butterfly (or imago, as the adult butterfly is known) breaks out of the cocoon, signalling the completion of the cycle. At first the wings are crumpled and small, but they soon expand and harden. About two hours after emerging, the imago is ready to fly. The imago is truly a delightsome beauty compared to the worm-like caterpillar. Unlike the ravaging caterpillar, the butterfly does not feed on green, leafy vegetation. That is too low class for it. At this stage, it prides itself on a high-class diet of nectar only. I suppose you could call the butterfly a 'nectarian'. It is a beautiful sight to watch the butterfly flapping gracefully as it flies from one flower to another in search of nectar. The butterfly is considered the friend of the farmer. This is because it helps in the process of cross-pollination as it flies from one flower to the other in search of nectar. This is a process vital for the reproduction of plants. So the life of a butterfly is a direct contrast to that of the destructive worm-like caterpillar whose main business is eating and destroying crops. That is why farmers consider the caterpillar an unwanted pest.

What is the lesson for us here? Every caterpillar is a potential butterfly. But, to metamorphose into a butterfly, it first has to go through the pupa stage where physiological development and changes have to take place. This crucial stage cannot be bypassed. There is no shortcut either. So, our caterpillar has two choices: submit itself totally to the process of inactivity in the puparium where it is cocooned and clinging onto a twig for support, or remain a worm and die as a worm without ever wearing the beautiful colours of a butterfly, or experiencing the thrills of flying among the flowers, or tasting the sweetness of nectar.

> *If you have great talent, industry will improve them;*
> *if you have but moderate abilities,*
> *industry will supply their deficiency.*[6]
> Sir Joshua Reynolds

You may be in your caterpillar stage – your early stage of development – right now. To blossom and metamorphose into a butterfly, you have to go through the pupa stage where your potential is developed. For your talents to amount to anything, they need developing, polishing, or fine-tuning. As a caterpillar, you are not of much use. You have to go through the pupa stage – the gym, training programme, skills development workshop, the university, music institute, a mentoring process or any other place or process where the best in you is refined, before you are presented to the world as an 'imago', a champion in your field of expertise. You can neither experience the thrills of rising to the top where your potential is at its best, nor taste the nectar of success and stardom without going through the pupa stage. The path to greatness must take you through some kind of puparium where you are groomed, trained, mentored, and polished, before you earn your badge of recognition.

There is no such thing as an instant celebrity. That is an illusion that belongs in the soap operas. Every celebrity had to pass through the pupa stage at some point in his or her career. This is the stage of training and transformation where skills and talents are developed and refined; the stage where new techniques of how to use those talents and skills, are acquired. This stage is a crucial stage that cannot be ignored or rushed if you are to achieve enduring success in your chosen field.

People seldom improve when they have no other model but themselves to copy. To be a successful painter, it often helps to train under the watchful eyes of another skilled and experienced master painter. Also, you don't become a graduate without going through a higher institution of learning where you acquire the necessary knowledge, skills, and mindset that prepare you for a successful career in your chosen field. That is the pupa stage. No one says it's easy. No one says it's a walk in the park. But it is absolutely necessary that you develop yourself daily to become your best if you are to get to the top and stay there.

So I ask you, which side of the show do you want to be on? The paying side or the earning side? If you don't develop yourself and put your gifts and talents to use, you will always be on the paying side. But if you somehow learn to develop and use even just ten per cent of your God-given abilities, you will always be on the earning side. People will pay to come and see you, hear you speak, watch you perform. And while you are simply enjoying doing what God has gifted you to do, the best part is that you are getting paid to do what you love to do.

Victory Starts Long Before the Event

The boxer who wins a title match does not necessarily win the match in the ring on the day of the bout. He merely goes into the ring to validate his victory and receive his title. His victory begins in the gym long before the actual bout: during the long, strenuous hours of training, practice, and learning new boxing techniques and perfecting old ones. That is where the victory is programmed before the actual event. The student who passes his professional examination does not achieve this feat on the day of the examination only. The victory begins long before the day of the actual event. It starts with the learning process in the classroom and in the library, and continues during the long hours of burning the midnight candle and studying hard over many days and months before the examination. That is how it works. Most people would rather have it another way – the easy way. They look at the long years of college education, the many strenuous hours of practice, the rigorous process of training and workouts, and the discipline of grooming their skills and talents under the tutelage of an experienced mentor and dismiss it as a waste of precious time. They forget that patience, discipline, and humility are indispensable qualities required to survive in the puparium. That is why their lives are hard. If you do what is easy now, you are setting yourself up for a hard life later. But if you do what is hard now, you are smoothing the way for an easy life later. Hard work is hard, that's why the majority of people try to avoid it. But in order for you to have what others don't have, you must be willing to do today the hard things that others won't do. If you aspire to be great in life, yet always tend to avoid doing what is necessary to get there because it is hard, I have news for you: there is no other way to become a butterfly. You must either submit totally to the transformative process in the puparium of life where your potential is forged in the crucible of hard work, discipline and humility, or you will remain a mediocre caterpillar the rest of your life without ever tasting the life of a butterfly. Period!

There are two ways to use your time: spend it, or invest it. Time spent in things of no enduring consequence is wasted time; but time invested in a worthy, purposeful, and profitable engagement is time redeemed. It always yields great returns. Therefore, any time spent in the puparium to develop yourself and enhance your mental, intellectual, physical, or spiritual shape has great consequence for your life and adds to the size of your future accomplishment. Invest your time. Don't spend it. Invest time to develop your mind. Do not waste all your time in front of the television screen changing channels and watching every movie or soap opera that pops up. Those people you are watching have emerged from their cocoons and are now living their dreams. Invest your time in developing yourself, in only reading, listening to, and watching materials that will help you grow and become a better person. If you increase your learning, you will develop your mind and, in turn, increase your earnings.

If you have made peace with the fact of the inevitability of the pupa stage in your journey to maximising your potential and becoming all that God wants you to be, then you must understand that this is a stage where you need to cling to the Lord as the pupa clings unto a twig. You need to rest in Him and trust Him for total support, protection, strength, and divine inspiration. He gave you the gifts and talents. He can help you to maximise them. This is the time when you cast all your cares and burdens upon the Lord, wait patiently on Him, and receive the comfort and encouragement that He gives as you go through the challenges of transformation and change from a caterpillar to a butterfly. The pupa stage is the refining stage where you pass through the heat that burns out the worst and brings out the best in you. It is the stage where you shed off the ugliness and negativity of the caterpillar in you and take on the nature of a champion. Believe me!

Joseph Went Through the Pupa Stage

From the time that Joseph, the son of Jacob, received his God-given dream for success till the time he became Prime Minister in Egypt, he had his fair share of refinement in the furnace of affliction. He was sold into slavery by his jealous brothers after being thrown into the pit of rejection. In the land of slavery in Egypt, he was thrown into the dungeon and locked away after being falsely accused of attempting to rape his master's wife. During all of these trials, which he endured patiently, clinging to the Lord all the way through, what Joseph didn't know was that each trial was a necessary ingredient that formed the recipe for his final promotion to the position of prime minister of Egypt. Every problem Joseph faced was part of the process designed to accelerate the process of accessing his promotion as prime minister. It was from prison that Joseph was transformed and summoned to the platform of glory. That was his puparium. It took a long time to get there. But that positional transformation would never have taken place if Joseph had not been cocooned in the dungeon where he had an opportunity to use his gift. If Nelson Mandela had not been kept in jail for twenty seven years by the apartheid government of South Africa, he would never have become a hero who came out of jail to become the first black president of South Africa. Even the Lord Jesus Christ Himself had to be crowned with thorns of affliction before he was crowned the King of kings and Lord of lords. There is no shortcut to glory. Take it from me!

Action Steps for Developing Your Potential

1.   Update your knowledge

Knowledge is a prized possession in the age and time that we live in. Phrases such as "you have to know something to become something" are popular with those who know through their own experiences the value of learning and knowledge. Knowledge has always been greatly valued, and the world is structured to accommodate those who study hard to be in the know. So, don't be satisfied with the way you are. You have to develop yourself creatively in every way possible. The French philosopher, Henri Bergson, once said that making progress was the key nature of life. Every living thing has to develop creatively; this is called the principle of life. It is necessary that you constantly watch your progress and exert yourself to become brighter, smarter, and better at whatever you do. If you don't update yourself, you will become outdated. One day, I walked into a large company and saw the company slogan which was very boldly written and hung outside for all to see. It read,

Yesterday we were good,

today we are better,

and tomorrow we want to be the best.

That is the spirit. If you don't improve in what you do, you will soon be disproved or outdone. If you hold a world record today and don't better it, someday someone will do better than you did, erase your record and set a new one. We have seen that happening over and over again.

Those who understand the importance of staying in touch with present and future developments and changes came up with the idea of continuous professional development and refresher courses to keep you at the cutting edge of the latest trends in your field. You will become an antiquated museum piece sooner than you know if you brush them aside and parade yourself only with outdated knowledge that you acquired in school twenty years ago. But you will do yourself a world of good if you are a regular at conferences, seminars, update courses, and workshops relevant to your area of expertise.

We have all been told that information is power, and those who have it have the edge. That is an indisputable fact. Having access to the right information at the right time gives you the edge. So, regular subscriptions to magazines and journals that will equip you with knowledge, information and skills that you need to improve yourself, develop your talents, and stay in touch with the rapid changes occurring daily in your field of interest, is a must.

> *If you are not constantly updated, you will be outdated.*
> *If you are not constantly inspired, you will gradually expire.*

2. *Your reading counts*

Your reading counts very much in updating your knowledge and improving yourself. There is an infamous saying in South Africa: "If you want to hide anything from a 'black man,' hide it in a book." I believe the idea behind this saying is that the 'black man' – a colloquial term for the unlearned – doesn't like reading books. That is why things that should be kept away from him, should be written in a book since he will never open it anyway. Let me quickly add here that 'blackness' is not necessarily a complexion of the skin. It is more of an attitude and the complexion of the mind. It is a characteristic mindset of someone who can read, should read, but won't read. So my advice to you is, don't be this so-called 'black man' who will not open a book to read. Be a wise man – read, read, and read. ***The more you read, the wiser and smarter you become***. But in reading, you must be careful what you feed your mind with. You must do away with trash and feed your mind only with material that is good, healthy, positive, spiritually and mentally enriching, and inspiring. Concentrate only on the very best. You will find the Bible particularly helpful. Also lay your hands on inspirational books, biographies, good educational materials, books that teach good business skills, communication skills, relationship skills, skills that will help you improve yourself in every way and develop your potential to the fullest. One elderly man has the habit of asking every young man he meets, "What book are you reading at the moment?" He understands that only those who develop themselves continuously through reading will make steady progress in life.

A few years ago, an 80-year-old American woman was featured in a TV news piece. What was amazing about this woman was not that she was 80, or that she was an American. The amazing thing about her that made her news headline was the simple fact that, even at 80 years of age, she decided to go back to university to earn a degree, something which, for some reason she couldn't do when she was much younger. Although becoming schoolmates with people the age of her grandchildren was not the easiest thing for this determined old woman to do, she was all the same very happy to be in school pursuing a degree. That was her life's ambition, and she was glad she could pursue her life-long dream. That was the beauty of it. What about Ruth, an Australian great grandmother who, at age 98 is still a competitive athlete? There is also Mrs. Magubane, the South African grandmother. She went to school at age 109 just to learn to read, write and sing from a hymn book – something she had always wanted to do.

She became South Africa's oldest graduate who graduated from a local college.

<blockquote>
Blessed is the man who has found his own work. Let him ask for no other blessing.
Unknown
</blockquote>

It is never too late. You have to be careful never to fall into the traps of excuses and rationalisation. Also, do not ever think that you have arrived yet. There is still so much to learn. The more you learn, the more you discover how much more there still is to learn. Never be satisfied with what you have achieved. There is always more that you can achieve. It was Thomas Edison who said, "There is a better way for everything. Find it." Never relax with second best. If you do not move, you become paralysed. If you don't develop all those gifts and talents that God has given to you, then you will develop a condition the doctors call agenesis. Keep moving forward till you reach your full potential. The moment you stop growing, you start dying. This is a fact of life. An abandoned and disused house will fall apart quicker than one that is occupied. A ship that is just sitting in the harbour will rot and leak much faster than one that is out there in the ocean cruising the continents of the world.

3.   Learn from a good role model

A role model is someone whose lifestyle and accomplishments inspire and motivate you. Good role models are leaders in their field and stand out because they have distinguished accomplishments credited to them. A good role model knows the way, has gone the way, and can show the way. Your role model should be someone whose dreams and life accomplishments are similar to what you plan to accomplish in life. This role model is the kind of person you want to become because he or she inspires courage and confidence in you.

To develop your potential and be all that God wants you to be, you need to find someone who has followed that path before. Where possible, arrange to meet and talk with people who are currently masters at doing what you want to do most, and are doing it well. Ask positive questions that will help you to learn all you can about their secrets to greatness. Find out how they started off in their career, what they did to grow and develop, what obstacles they faced and what they did to overcome setbacks during their learning curve. Let them share with you what they did to stay positive, focused, and motivated. Where it is not possible to meet with them or attend lectures and talks given by them personally, buy and listen to their tapes and videos, read their books and any other material written by or about them. Reading their biographies or autobiographies is particularly helpful. Find out how they struggled through life, how they lived, and what they did to overcome all odds to get to where they are. Where it is at all possible to personally meet with your role model, by all means make an appointment to do so as soon as you can. Good role models are humble and modest in spite of their achievements, and they are always flattered to know that there's someone out there who thinks they are heroes and who wants to come and learn a thing or two from them. Good role models are always willing to guide and to help you become your best if you ask them.

At the Tshwane University of Technology, South Africa, the following has been written on the wall of the foyer at the Centre for Continuous Professional Development:

To be able to soar way above mediocrity and
touch the sky, you need to get a strong eagle that
will carry you under its wings.
When the eagle releases you, the chances of
falling will be nil because you shall have learned
from a real mentor, an eagle.

4.   *Start using your gifts and talents*

The more you put your gifts and talents to use, the more they develop, and as you develop and use them, you will discover more of your gifts. No matter how little you think they are right now, determine to develop them through the discipline of training, and by putting them to regular use. Practice makes perfect. As you cultivate and use them, they will grow and become more refined and more developed. You become better by doing; ask any swimmer. A child who learns to walk does so by constant practice, by not being afraid to fall, and by his willingness to keep trying in spite of the risk of falling. To develop your potential and become all that God wants you to be, just begin by doing the little you can the best way you can. That is about all it takes for your potential to start growing. It's really all about doing: the more you do, the more you improve and set yourself up for success. If you fail at the beginning, don't get discouraged and give up. The tortoise never makes any headway without sticking its neck out. You may risk being ridiculed by mediocre people who sit by and attempt nothing. You may even come under sharp criticism by people who are bereft of vision. But keep on keeping on. Do not tire of doing your best. You will reap the benefits in due time if you do not faint. Remember, the journey of a thousand miles begins with a step. Take that first step now. Art L. Williams wrote a book he titled *All You Can Do Is All You Can Do But All You Can Do Is Enough!*[7] I say to you, whatever you do under God's blue heavens, make sure you do all you can do.

5.   *Build up your self-confidence*

Your degree of self-confidence is crucial to developing your potential. If you do not believe in yourself, nobody else will believe in you. God has given you the gifts and abilities to be your best. The fact that your potential is still in the process of development is not an excuse to belittle yourself before people with obvious, well-developed potential. Resist the temptation to compare yourself with others; if you do you will sink yourself in the quicksand of an inferiority complex which will stand between you and the best that God intends for you. You do not have to be able to do the same things as your peers to feel good about yourself. You are unique, with a unique set of gifts and abilities, and a unique purpose in life. God has given you all it takes to fulfil your unique purpose in life. Concentrate on fulfilling your purpose. Be the best you can be. Don't try to be someone else. It is better to be the original of yourself than to be the photocopy of someone else. Believe in yourself and others will believe in you. Other times though, as you struggle with your self-worth, it may so happen that there is someone who believes in you, even though you are not yet in that space where you feel very confident about yourself. At least believe in that person's belief in you, until your belief in yourself kicks in.

6.   *Be enthusiastic about your potential*

Enthusiasm has been described as the gasoline that drives things forward. It is your enthusiasm and faith combined that will keep you going in times of adversity, failure, temporary setback, ridicule and discouragement. When you are enthusiastic about what you do, you can overcome both physical and mental fatigue more easily than someone who is not. The German philosopher Nietzsche once said, "Nothing ever succeeds which exuberant spirits have not helped to produce." This is true even for success in developing your potential. If you recognise your potential and believe in it, then being enthusiastic about it will help you develop it and grow it big. No one ever made headway in life without a strong passion for what he does. Talk about your gifts and talents with enthusiasm. Pursue your area of calling with passion. When you do, your enthusiasm and passion will groom, brighten and refine your potential.

Stir Them All Up

The apostle Paul had a few people who worked very closely with him. Some of them he referred to as his children. Timothy was one of them. This was a young man who was prone to timidity because of his age and circumstances. But he was a gifted young man who later became a bishop. Paul was his spiritual father and mentor, and he often wrote to him to encourage him in the work of the Lord.

In one of his letters to Timothy, Paul wrote:

*...I would remind you to **stir up** (rekindle the embers of, fan the flame of, and keep burning) the (gracious) **gift of God**, (the inner fire) that is **in you** by means of the laying on of my hands (with those of the elders at your ordination).* (2 Tim 1:6 AMP).

At the time of his ordination, Timothy received special gifts of the Spirit to enable him serve the church and fulfil his role as a bishop. In 1 Tim. 4:14, Paul reminds him of the gift which he received by divine prophetic impartation: *Do not neglect the **gift that is in you**, which was given to you by prophecy with the laying on of hands of the eldership.* (NKJV)

In reminding Timothy to '***stir up***' those gifts, Paul was not only implying that there is a possibility of those gifts remaining dormant and unproductive, but he was also stating in clear terms that those gifts were like inner coals of fire whose embers must be fanned to keep them alive, active, and flaming. In like manner, if live coals of fire are left unfanned, with time they begin to lose their flaming power, and the intensity of heat they produce gradually reduces. They start to smoulder, become cold and eventually die.

God has put some gifts in you that you need to be reminded of so you can stir them all up. The word 'to stir' means to arouse, to excite, or to stimulate. The gifts in you need to be aroused, excited, and stimulated. These gifts are like ingredients in water that can only be properly mixed together by stirring. They are also like sediments in a liquid. To rise up from the bottom of the liquid to the top, they must be stirred. So, never allow your gifts to remain at the bottom; bring them to the top by stirring them up so they can be developed. Exercise your gifts, talk about them, put them to use, and be open to opportunities to showcase them. That way, the embers of your gifts will remain kindled. You've got it in there in you; stir it, fan it, excite it and bring it to the fore!

Let me conclude this chapter with the following story:

Pastor William F. Kumuyi, the general overseer of the *Deeper Christian Life Ministry*, is one of the most outstanding and well respected men of God in Africa. As a growing young boy in school, he was the kind of student one would look at as a write-off. His attitude towards school was that of complete nonchalance. He couldn't care less whether he passed or failed. When other students were busy paying attention in class or studying hard, he was either busy fighting or playing with like-minded friends in school and throwing away his life. His father got tired of him, took one long look at him and concluded the boy was a failure. But the turning point came when the young William sat down one day and decided it was time to take stock of his life. He decided it was time to stop fooling around, get serious with his life, his career, his future, and to have a complete change of attitude toward his studies. He became serious with his life and started stirring up all the gifts and talents in him. That one moment of a complete turn-around changed his life forever. He went on to become a mathematician and lectured at the University of Lagos before he went into full-time ministry as the founder and senior pastor of the *Deeper Christian Life Ministry*. The *Deeper Life Bible Church* has become one of the largest and fastest growing churches in Nigeria and has planted many branches all over Nigeria, and in many countries abroad. Pastor Kumuyi is an outstanding teacher of God's Word, an author of many books and a well-respected and gifted minister both in the African continent and beyond. His Lagos-based ministry has trained and raised thousands of pastors and missionaries through the *International Bible Training College* which he founded.

Paul said to Timothy, *Do not neglect the gift that is in you...rekindle the embers of, fan the flames of, and keep burning the gift of God (inner fire) that is in you.*

Until you stir up the gift of God in you, you will never be the best that God wants you to be.

BE THE BEST OF WHATEVER YOU ARE

If you can't be a pine on the top of a hill,
Be a shrub in the valley
But be the best little shrub
At the side of the road.
Be a bush if you can't be a tree.

We can't all be captains,
Some have to be crew.
There's something for all of us here;
There's work to be done and
We've all got to do our part on the way that's sincere

If you can't be a highway,
Then just be a trail;
If you can't be a sun, be a star,
It isn't by size that you win or you fail.
Be the best of whatever you are.

Author Unknown

POINTS TO PONDER

- Refuse to be counted among people with very good brains and extremely creative minds who are living a wasted life in the slum of mediocrity because they failed to use their creative minds creatively and profitably.
- You can neither experience the thrills of rising to the top where your potential is at its best, nor taste the nectar of success and stardom without going through the pupa stage.
- Either submit totally to the transformative process in the puparium of life where your potential is forged in the crucible of hard work, discipline, and humility, or remain a mediocre caterpillar the rest of your life without ever tasting the life of a butterfly.
- The pupa stage is the refining stage when you pass through the heat that burns out the worst and brings out the best in you.
- The more you put your gifts and talents to use, the more they develop, and the more gifts you will discover.
- Until you stir up the gift of God in you, you will never be the best that God wants you to be.
- If you don't believe in yourself, no one will believe in you.

> *Successful people use their strength by recognising, developing, and utilising the talents of others.*
> Zig Ziglar

APPLICATION ACTIVITIES

1. Which of your talents are well developed? List them below.

    a.

    b.

    c.

2. Name those talents that need to be incubated and developed further.

    a.

    b.

    c.

3. What are you going to do about each of them and when?

4. Which three persons could you approach to help you develop your talents?

    a.

    b.

    c.

Chapter Five
USE YOUR POTENTIAL

If a man has a talent and cannot use it, he has failed.
If he has a talent and uses only half of it, he has partly failed.
If he has a talent and learns somehow to use the whole of it, he has
gloriously succeeded, and won a satisfaction and a triumph few men
ever know.
Thomas Wolfe

Developing all your gifts and talents, and successfully putting them to use in reaching your fullest potential, is truly a great experience. There is great satisfaction in seeing yourself doing what you love to do best, and doing it in an outstanding way. Whether it be in athletics, academia, music, sculpture, or sports, it is always fulfilling to be all that God wants you to be, and to do what you enjoy doing best. Therein lies peace, therein lies contentment, and therein lies joy and true success.

The more of your potential you are able to discover, develop, and put to use, the more of a blessing you will be to humanity, and the more successful you will become in life.

Consider the story of Amelia Earhart. She was a woman who combined many talents in her pursuit of excellence. She became the first woman aviator to cross the Atlantic. She was an author, an entrepreneur, a nurse and a fashion designer. One edition of *FORTUNE* magazine published in Lagos wrote the following about Amelia Earhart:

Some say things can't be done. Others do them, proving that with the right combination of bravado and talent, there is no telling what you can accomplish.

Nicknamed 'Lady Lindy,' Amelia Earhart was not only the first woman to fly solo across the Atlantic, she held women's speed and distance records that earned her a place as the first woman to receive the Distinguished Flying Cross.

As a nurse during World War 1, Earhart developed an early concern for her fellow man that helped her champion human rights around the world. Her memorable accomplishments in the air moved her to pen three best-selling books.

She served as aviation editor for Cosmopolitan. *She designed and marketed a line of luggage and founded two successful airlines. An admired poet, she inspired two popular songs and even a foxtrot aptly called the Earhart Hop.*

Her adventurous lifestyle so enthralled the American people that she created fashions for top department stores like Macy's and Marshall Field's.[8]

The life of Amelia Earhart is the epitome of what it means to combine many talents in the pursuit of excellence. That is one of the primary objectives of this book – to plant your feet firmly on the pathway of success and achievement by uncovering and maximising all your potential.

The most celebrated artist of the Italian Renaissance, Michelangelo Buonarroti, was a man who discovered his artistic talents early in life, and somehow learnt to use most of it to the fullest. His genius was expressed not only as a sculptor and painter, but also a poet, architect, and military engineer. His skilled hands made statues that seem to breathe, paintings that are art-museum treasures, and buildings that are breathtaking in their magnificence.

Most people never achieve anything in life, not because they haven't got talent, not even because they don't know they've got talent, but most times the problem is due to laziness, procrastination and the fear of failure. No one succeeds who never tries anything, who postpones till another 'convenient' time what could have been done today, or who decides not to get started until the fear of the possibility of failure is completely eliminated.

When the former American basketball legend, Michael Jordan, first resigned from the game of basketball and decided to go into baseball in October 1993, someone asked him if he thought he could be as successful in baseball as he was in basketball. He quickly replied: "I am not afraid of failing, but I cannot afford not to try. Defeat is not failure unless you pronounce it to be."

We have all heard about Thomas Edison and his many experiments, his failures, and his eventual success. He made the lesson of his life clear when he noted that most people miss an opportunity because it is dressed in overalls and looks like work. Most of the work is in developing your potential. When you learn to use your developed potential in the spirit of love by helping the people around you and making a difference in the world, the doors of success have no choice but to fly open before you. This success in its dormant stage is called opportunity, and it resides in you in its seed form as potential. When developed and put to use, there is no telling what things you can do, what heights you can reach, or what mountains you can conquer. Richard Byrd puts it this way: "Few men in their life time come anywhere near exhausting the resources dwelling within them. There are deep wells of strength that are never used."

He Turned His Scars into Stars

During the 1996 Paralympics in Atlanta, USA, a disabled Nigerian athlete, Ajibola Adeoye, won two gold medals and one silver medal. In athletics, he won gold in both the 100m and 200m events, and a silver medal in long jump. All three were records of sort: world record in both track events, and a personal record in long jump, an event he had never participated in before. But that was not all. Previously, Ajibola had won gold medals in Barcelona Paralympics in 1992, in Cairo's All African Game in 1991 and 1995, and London's meet for the disabled in 1991 and 1993.

Ajibola's journey into the sprint world started when he was discovered in school as a runner at age 13. This was 7 years after an accident that caused one of his arms to be amputated by doctors who told his parents his life was at risk.

But physical disability was not all that he had to contend with. Beyond his disability, another thing that could have held him down was poverty. The day after their return from Atlanta, families, friends, and journalists thronged his home to throw him a most deserved welcome party. Opening a window into the state of poverty out of which Ajibola fought his way to win these Paralympic gold medals, one of the journalists who was at his home later reported:

The room and parlour inhabited by his family in a rented bungalow in Iyana-Ipaja, Lagos, wore lowliness like a deep tribal mark. Weather-beaten calendar and family photographs adorn the wall, a foot-worn carpet graced the floor, three shabby, upholstered chairs provided seats. No radio; no television; or other necessities of modern living. The parlour was creaking under the weight of human presence, as the grubby cloth that curtained the parlour from the room kept falling off, revealing winks of the two wooden beds crowding the room.[9]

Ajibola fought through poverty and disability to put his name in history books as an achiever, a winner, and a star. With this feat, this one-arm amputee, who was previously unknown and unsung, shot into the limelight and achieved a feat most able-bodied young men with both arms and both feet complete have not achieved, because he dared to put his talents to use.

If he can do it, why can't you? Don't hold back anymore. Begin to unleash your potential if you want to get ahead and make your mark. Like Ajibola, you can turn your scars into stars. Aristotle wrote:

As in the Olympic Games, it is not the most beautiful and strongest who receive the crown, but those who actually enter the combat, for from those came the victors, so it is those who act that win rightly what is noble and good in life.

If you ever find yourself saying that you are too old to pursue your dreams, or too scared to do something noble that you've always wanted to do, then you must recognise that you are now listening to the negative voice inside of you that has been responsible for holding you back and keeping you down all these years. That voice is not your friend, so you must sternly issue a warning to it to "shut up, and back off!" Remind that voice of all the many people who started their lives all over again at any age they wanted to, and they went on to achieve their dreams. Tell that voice to go look for someone else to deceive because you have made up your mind to achieve your dreams. And absolutely nothing, not even a negative voice in your head, can stop you from succeeding in life. If you can do that every time that negative voice shows up knocking on your doorstep and telling you what you can or cannot do, then you are liberated from what holds other people back seventy per cent of the time from fulfilling their dreams.

The Ideal Coach

The man who would make a good coach, in my opinion, would not be the man who has a brilliant game plan, who knows what to do and what not to do. He would not be the man who claims to have a winning formula or a super strategy to win the game. I believe a good coach would be the man who, at some time, has been in the game himself; a man who has himself experienced the thrills of victory and the agony of defeat; a man who coaches, not because he has seen it done somewhere, but because he has experienced it himself. He is the man who knows the way, has gone the way, and can show the way. He is the man who coaches, not from what he learnt from school, or what he read in a book, but from his experience as one who has been in the arena as an active player in the game he coaches. There is a big difference between knowing the path and walking the path. How much a man knows is of no importance; what matters is what he does with what he knows. I submit that a good coach would be that man who, in the ring of play, has given his blood, sweat and tears to build a reputation in his field. It is easy for just about anyone to be an armchair critic, a self-appointed analyst sitting on the side-lines and pointing out how something should have been done better. Anyone can sit back in the comfort of their inactivity and laugh at those who stumble or fail trying to engrave their names in the history books. But

President Theodore Roosevelt, in one of his famous quotes, describes who the true hero is:

It is not the critic who counts, not the man who points out how the strong man stumbled, or where the doer of deeds could have done it better. The credit belongs to the man who is actually in the arena; whose face is marred by dust and sweat and blood; who strives valiantly; who errs and comes short again and again; who knows the great enthusiasm, the great devotions, and spends himself in a worthy cause; who, at best, knows in the end the triumph of high achievement; and who, at the worst, if he fails, at least fails while daring greatly, so that his place shall never be with those cold and timid souls who know neither victory nor defeat.

Use It or Lose It

To every one of us God has given gifts and talents. He did not give them to us to hang on the wall as trophies. He gave them to us for productivity and service, and so that we can contribute towards making our world better than we found it. According to the law of use, whatever you don't use, you lose. This law is clearly illustrated by Jesus in the Bible when He told the parable of the talents in Matthew 25:14-30. In this parable, a master called his three servants together one day and told them he was going on a journey and will be gone for a while. But before he left, he gave five talents to the first servant, two talents to the second servant, and one talent to the third, according to their different abilities. "Take these talents and see what you can do with them," he said to them. "When I come back from my journey we shall get together again and go over the books to see what you have done with the talents," he told them. "Ok," said the servants." Then the master took off.

According to the story, when the master got back, he called together all three servants, and as he said he would, he asked them how they each fared with the talents he gave them.

"You gave me five talents," said the first servant. "I put those talents to work, and I doubled them from five to ten. That is a 100 per cent profit. Here, the books will show it." The master was impressed and commended the servant for his hard work and faithfulness in service.

"You gave me two talents," said the second servant to his master. "I also put them to work and gained two more talents, making four in total." The master was impressed. "You have also done very well," he commended, and he promised, "For your being faithful with the little you were given, you will also get a promotion."

Then came the servant who received one talent. "I gave you one talent," said the master. "What did you do with it?" The servant responded, "Master, I took the one talent you gave me, dug a hole and hid it carefully where no one would find it. So when I heard you were back from your journey, I went back to the spot where I hid it and dug up the talent. Fortunately, nothing happened to it. Here it is, carefully wrapped, exactly the way you gave it to me."

According to the story, the master was not happy with this servant, instead of being commended like the others, the master said, "Take that talent away from him and give it to the servant who has ten talents." The master went on to say, "To him who has, more shall be given. But to him who has not, even the one which he has shall be taken away."

That, my friend, is called the 'law of use.' Lack of use causes loss. What you don't use today, you lose. Be it time, talent, abilities, virtue or vitality. Whatever you do not employ and put to use, you forfeit. If you use the abilities you've been given, God will increase them by helping you to discover even more. If you fail to use what you've been given, you will lose them. Speaking to his protégé Timothy about this, the apostle Paul said, *Be sure to use the abilities God has given you…. Put these abilities to work.* (1 Tim. 4:14-15 Living Bible). You were meant to exhaust your potential here on earth. If you die with all that potential in you, you will enrich the grave and deprive the world by failing to empty upon her your all.

Medical doctors, physiotherapists and body builders all strongly agree that the more you exercise your muscles, the more they develop and become stronger; if the muscles remain unused for some time, they begin to weaken and waste away. This condition is termed *disuse atrophy*. In the same way, the more you use your God-given abilities, the more they develop; the more you fail to use them, the more they weaken and atrophy. The Lord Jesus knew this quite well when he said, *Every branch in me that beareth not fruit he taketh away; and every branch that beareth fruit, he purgeth it, that it may bring forth more fruit.* (John 15:2)

Practice Makes Perfect

Whatever gifts you have been given can be enlarged and refined through constant use. No one, for instance, becomes an expert driver overnight. Skill comes with practice – constant practice. No one becomes a great swimmer by reading great books about swimming. It takes constant practice in the pool to be a great swimmer. So it is with the gift of teaching. With practice, constant study and feedback, a good teacher can become a better teacher, and with time, will grow to be a master teacher. Extraordinary men were simply ordinary men who kept doing little things in little ways, and with time, grew and learnt how to do them in extraordinary ways. Great opportunities often disguise themselves in little things. Before attempting the extraordinary, you can start by doing the small, ordinary things. With time, persistence and determination, your great break will come. Temporary setbacks should be expected. That is normal. But only you, by your response and attitude to them, can make them either a permanent defeat or a stepping stone to greatness.

Never let another day pass without doing the right thing, now that you know what to do. Many people have a good aim in life but never pull the trigger. Some never accomplish anything because they never got started. Refuse to be another addition to statistics. Some of the most talented singers are never heard. Some of the most talented footballers and athletes never make a team. Reason? Failure to develop their talents into a quality, disciplined performance. Others look for the easy way, the shortcut, and fail to pay the price through constant practice. Still others put off what should be done today till some other convenient time – a time that never seems to arrive. Procrastination and hesitation are twin demons that together have conspired and strangulated more dreams, more good intentions, and more worthy goals and aspirations than anything else I can think of. Consider how the poet Evangeline Wilkes puts it:

On the sands of hesitation
Lay the bones of countless millions,
Who at the dawn of victory
Sat down to wait,
And waiting – died!

Don't just store up your potential and refuse to express it. The Dead Sea is situated at the lowest point on earth at 430.5 metres below sea level. Due to its geographical location below sea level, water only flows into it but never flows out. That is why it is referred to as 'Dead Sea' because, with a salt content of 35 per cent, almost 9 times saltier than the ocean, its harsh environment is not conducive to either plant or animal life. If you don't want to lose your talents, rise up and start using them right now. Don't wait for when the time is right, or when there is no risk of failure. There is absolutely nothing wrong if you fail a few times on your way up. Just get started from somewhere – anywhere. The journey of a thousand miles begins with a single step. Take that step right now. It is in *doing*, in the discipline of practice, that a violinist becomes a master.

Consider the following poem, a paraphrase of a verse that speaks of one of the most tragic lives ever lived on this planet:

OPPORTUNITIES MISSED

There was a very cautious man
Who never laughed or played
He never risked, he never tried

He never sang or prayed
And when he one day passed away
His insurance was denied
For since he never really lived
They claimed he never died.

Author Unknown

A famous educator once said that we should do the things we love doing and can do well. Only then will we start to realise that we are able to experience fulfilment to an infinitely greater extent than we ever thought possible. You want to be an actor, start acting; you want to be a singer, start singing; you want to be an Olympic medallist in swimming, get into the pool and start practising; you want to be a successful writer, pick up your pen and start writing. That was what I told myself before I wrote this book. Once I started, everything I needed to complete the book began to come to me. Of course I made a few mistakes here and there, but the more I wrote, the better it got. Don't wait till everything is right – it may never be. Almost everything we do is done poorly when we first start. That is how we learn. Don't stop trying! Keep doing what you do badly until you can do it right!! You don't have to be great to get started; but you cannot be great if you don't get started. So push that start button NOW!

It's All About Using

Joseph used his gift of dreams and he saved the nation from famine and became a prime minister in Egypt. David used his gift of music and he was brought to sing in the king's palace; again, he used his gift of faith and he brought down Goliath of Gath, the dreaded Philistine giant. Bezaleel and Aholiab used their gifts of architecture and design and they built a tabernacle for the Lord. Timothy was reminded to stir up the gifts in him; he did and became a bishop. Elijah used his gift of prayer and he controlled the weather, fire and kings. Elisha used his gift of prophecy and even in death his dead bones raised a dead man who was thrown into his tomb. The Shunammite woman used her gift of hospitality and her womb was opened and she had a son. The woman with the issue of blood exercised her little gift of faith and she was healed without charge or side effects. Peter used his gift of eloquence after the Pentecost experience and 5000 men were saved in one day. Abraham used his gift of faith and he became the father of many nations. Paul used his gift of writing and he gave us the 13 Pauline Epistles. Solomon used his gift of poetry and he gave us the books of Proverbs, Ecclesiastes and Songs of Solomon. Be ashamed to die until you have made your contribution to humanity.

God has given you the gift of life. What you make out of life is up to you. No one else can ever take your place or do the things God has created you to do for humanity. If you fail to make your unique contribution to your generation, no one else will do it for you. You cannot outsource your unique mandate to your generation. No one else can use your voice for you, or use your other skills and abilities for you. Never again should you open your mouth to say that you don't have anything to offer, that you are not gifted, or that God created you with a little less than the usual something He has given to everyone else who is achieving. Many studies conducted have shown that the average person is endowed with between 500 and 700 different abilities. Just to give you an idea what is locked up inside you, your brain can store 100 trillion facts. Your mind can handle 15,000 decisions a second, as is the case when your digestive system is working. Your nose can smell up to 10,000 different odours. Your touch can detect an item 1/25,000[th] of an inch thick, and your tongue can taste one part of quinine in 2 million parts of water. Never again should you hide under the excuse that you don't have any gifts you can use to make a visible difference. The greatest risk in life is not to take any risk at all. If you are not unleashing your potential, if you are not involved in any service where you are making a difference, what excuses are you still hiding behind? Don't be a benchwarmer on this earth. You were not created just to exist and occupy space. You live for a purpose – to make a difference. If you fail to do it, you would have lived a wasted life, and would have wasted God's resources. Consider the following poem:

A BAG OF TOOLS

Isn't it strange
That princes and kings,
And clowns that caper
In sawdust rings,
And common people
Like you and me
Are builders for eternity?
Each is given a bag of tools,
A shapeless mass,
A book of rules;
And each must make -
Ere life is flown -
A stumbling block
Or a stepping stone.
R.L. Sharpe

Now that you know that you have potential, now that you recognise the need to develop your unique sets of gifts and talents and put them to use for the service of God and humanity, and now that you understand that what you do not use, you lose, what are you waiting for?

POINTS TO PONDER

- The more of your potential you are able to discover, develop, and put to use, the more value you will add to humanity, and the more successful and fulfilled you will become in life.
- No one succeeds who never tries anything, who postpones till another 'convenient' time what could have been done today, or who decides not to get started until the fear of the possibility of failure is completely eliminated.
- The man who would make a great coach….is the man who knows the way, has gone the way, and can show the way.
- The more you use your God-given abilities, the more they develop; the more you fail to use them, the more they weaken and atrophy.
- Many people have a good aim in life but they never pull the trigger. Some never accomplish anything because they never got started.
- Don't wait till everything is right – it may never be. Almost everything we do is done poorly when we first start. That is how we learn.
- Don't stop trying! Keep doing what you do badly until you can do it right!!
- You don't have to be great to get started, but you cannot be great if you don't get started. So push that start button NOW!

> *I hope that the day I appear in front of God,*
> *I will have no talent left and that I will be able to say:*
> *'God, I have used all the talents you gave me.'*
> Erma Bombeck

APPLICATION ACTIVITIES

1. List below important projects you wish to undertake but have not started. Remember, the journey of a thousand miles begins with a step.
   (a). Project 1:……………………………………………………………
   (b). Project 2:…………………………………………………...……….

2. What are the projects you have started, but have not completed, or have abandoned? Pick out those projects now and finish them.
   (a) Project 1:……………………………………….……………...
   (b) Project 2:……………………………………………...........................

3. What resources do you need to complete the projects and how are you going to get them?
   (a) Project 1 resources:……………………………..............................
       How to get them:…………………………………….....:………..
   (b) Project 2 resources:……………………………...........................
       How to get them:……………………………………......………..

4. Write down a date by which each project must be completed.
   (a) Project 1 estimated completion date:………...............................
   (b) Project 2 estimated completion date:………..................................

5. How will you reward yourself for each project successfully completed?
   (a) Project 1 reward:……………………………...............................
   (b) Project 2 reward:……………………………...............................

Chapter Six

YOU ARE NOT INFERIOR

What you know, the same do I know also;
I am not inferior unto you.
Job 13:2

You are probably familiar with the popular joke about the American who tried to patronise a Japanese delegate during the farewell dinner at an international television conference in the U.S.A. After the Japanese had finished his soup, the American who was sitting next to him turned to him and asked, "Likee soupee?" The Japanese gentleman nodded without saying a word. Throughout the meal the American kept asking the Japanese such questions as, "Likee fishee?" and "Likee drinkee?"

When the meal was finally over, the chairman of the conference got up and introduced this same Japanese gentleman as the guest speaker of the meeting. The Oriental gentleman gave a witty, excellent speech on the future of broadcasting – speaking much better English than any American had ever uttered. After his speech, the Japanese gentleman returned to his seat and, turning to his American table companion, asked, "Likee speechee?"

One great lesson I have learnt over the years is never to put anyone down or treat them condescendingly, no matter how small or unimportant they look. Everyone has enormous hidden potential, whether it is apparent to us or not. It was Johann Wolfgang van Goethe who admonished, "Look at a man the way that he is, he only becomes worse. But look at him as if he were what he could be, then he becomes what he should be." I guess what Goethe is trying to tell us is that what we often see is usually not all that there is. What we see is just the tip of the iceberg compared to what there really is. Goethe is also implying that a man should not be measured merely by what he has presently accomplished, but by what he is capable of accomplishing with his abilities fully developed. The person you look down upon today and write off as unimportant, unintelligent, or incapable may end up becoming your boss tomorrow. The man you dismiss and throw in jail today because of his political views may come out tomorrow to be your president. Ask Nelson Mandela. Ask Olusegun Obasanjo. They both know exactly what I am talking about. The fact that someone is small in some way today does not mean he will remain like that forever. *Let no one despise or think less of you because of your youth,* was Paul's charge to Timothy in 1 Timothy chapter 4 verse 12 (Amp).

Successful Artists Who Were Rejected

Countless numbers of artists and actors who are very successful today were turned down during their first auditions. Most of them were turned down for lack of talent by short-sighted men who looked at the now and failed to see what these young men and women were capable of becoming.

Pastor Martins Balogun, who started off his music career with his popular stage name of Broda Martins, is a celebrated Nigerian gospel musician of *Musin Olosa* fame. He is one of such artists who were turned down at an audition. Broda Martins invited me (the author) to join him at the recording studio on 2nd of August 1994 while he was working on the voice sampling of his album *Double Edge*. As we walked down to the studio, I asked him how he began his music career, and he told me his story.

When he discovered his talent in music, he became interested in joining his church choir where he thought he could develop it, put it to regular use and become a blessing to the church. He made his interest known and was invited for auditioning. When he went for the audition, without even giving him a chance to try, the music director just took one look at him and said to him, "Sorry, I don't think you are the kind of person we are looking for. The standard of this choir is high and we are looking for people who can sing very well."

Broda Martins was turned down because they merely looked at him and concluded that he couldn't sing and did not even deserve to be given a chance.

Broda Martins went away disappointed, but not discouraged. He left, but he didn't quit. He knew he had what it takes, even though the music director thought otherwise.

Some time went by, and Broda Martins found himself in another church that was forming a new choir. The music director of this new church sent out invitations for interested vocalists to come for auditioning. That was the chance Broda had been waiting for.

During the auditioning, the vocalists were called up one by one to sing a song, while the pianist played in the background. So, one by one each of the vocalists stepped forward to show the stuff they had. Finally it was the turn of Broda Martins. He sang a song titled *I will celebrate*. He sang this song so well that the keyboardist decided to test his voice further. He changed the keys, modulated, and Broda Martins flowed so well that everyone went wow! They were so impressed that one of the men in the audition who had come from the previous church where he was turned down said, "Balogun (that's his surname), so you can sing like this and we didn't know all this time!"

That was just the beginning for Broda Martins. With that song, he celebrated his way into fame. Today, Broda Martins has about 12 successful gospel music albums in the market, including the album *Mushin Olosha* for which he is well known. Apart from being the founding pastor of the *Whole Armour Ministries*, also known as *The Triumphant Garrison Church* (or *TriGar Family Church*), he also runs a weekly praise seminar for choristers and music ministers. He has also established a music school, *The Ekklesia Music Institute*, where young musicians are trained and helped to develop their musical talents. He is an artist, a painter, poet, author, actor, song-writer and composer. His multiple talents are also expressed in his ability to play many musical instruments including the guitar, saxophone, keyboard, and drums. He has received numerous awards including The Christian Music Award, CBAN Award and the

Kingdom Music Award, for his outstanding contributions to gospel music in Nigeria.

Another woman who tasted the bitter pill of rejection at her first audition was Madame Ernestine Schumann-Heink (1861-1936). She was a famous American operatic contralto known for the size, beauty, tonal richness, flexibility, and wide range of her voice, and has been described as one of the most beloved singers of all times. Her story is captured in the following short paragraph of a news dispatch:

Early in her career, Mme. Schumann-Heink visited the director of the Vienna Court Opera, to have him test her voice. But he did not test it. After taking one look at the awkward and poorly dressed girl, he exclaimed, none too gently, "With such a face, and no personality at all, how can you ever expect to succeed in opera? My good child, give up the idea. Buy a sewing machine, and go to work. You can never be a singer."[10]

Never is a long time! The Vienna Court Opera director knew much about the technique of singing, but he obviously knew little about the corked, waiting-to-be-released potential. He used his 'episcope' pretty well on Mme Schumann-Heink, but he failed to use his 'endoscope'. If he had looked as he should do, he would have seen something waiting to be released in her, and would not have condemned genius without giving it an opportunity. Mme. Schumann-Heink proved this Opera director wrong and became a famous contralto in the world of opera.

They Called Him a Babbler

Paul the apostle was a very remarkable man as we all know. But, as remarkable as he was, there were certain people who looked at him and wrote him off before even hearing what he had to say.

While he was waiting in Athens for his two companions, Silas and Timothy, to join him, Paul went to the synagogue for discussions with the Jews and the devout Gentiles, and spoke daily in the public square to all who happened to be there. But he had an encounter with some learned men, and their first impression about him was recorded in Acts 17:18 as follows: *Then certain philosophers of the Epicureans, and of the Stoics, encountered him. And some said, "What will this babbler say…"*

A 'babbler.' That is what they thought of him. Paul was prejudiced against and judged even before he was allowed to say a word. Many people make the mistake of judging others before giving them a chance or hearing what they have to say. Very often, people are judged based on their physical appearance, skin colour, race, tribe, culture, social status, or some other external criteria. Unknown to these ignorant learned men, they were referring to a man who had a unique encounter with Jesus Christ, a fine lawyer who trained under Gamaliel – one of the most respected members of the Sanhedrin, the highest judicial body in Jerusalem, a man who had, tucked inside of him, all 13 *Pauline Epistles* waiting to go to press, a man who turned cities and nations upside down with his powerful, life-changing messages; a man whose writings would positively affect many generations in every corner of the world, even thousands of years after he was gone. Such was the man that stood before them. Unfortunately, because of their ignorance and tunnel-vision, all they could see was a poor, little babbler who was a little short of being an object of caricature, a sure pointer to the fact that their 'endoscope' was not only out of focus, but obsolete and dead.

Never underrate or underestimate anyone because of how they look without giving them a chance. Looks could be deceiving. Over the years, I have observed that many so-called babblers, write-offs, and dunces often have very meaningful and important contributions to make to society. It is a great mistake to write people off because of social status, race, colour, or background, without giving them a chance to try.

Many 'babblers' have ruled nations, turned the tide of history, saved entire nations from shame and destruction… because somehow, someone believed in them and gave them the opportunity to try. Saul could easily have dismissed David as a loafer and charged him with bluffing when he offered to take on Goliath. But Saul gave him a chance and risked allowing him to conquer the giant and save Israel, or lose and bring the nation to disrepute and servitude. If David had been refused the opportunity to take on the giant, the reproach of defeat and the damage of failure in battle would have been irreparable for Israel.

Many men and women have remained mediocre and given up on all attempts at reaching lofty heights because someone, somewhere, told them something like these: "Come on boy, you can't sing, so stop fooling around", or, "don't waste your time kid, give it up, only intelligent people go on to medical school, not people like you", or, "don't go and make a fool of yourself, you haven't got what it takes, the opera is not for people like you." They believed those mentally crippling words to their own undoing.

It is time to wake up. It's not too late to pursue your dreams. You can continue right now from where you left off. Never again should you allow anyone to talk you into a state of perpetual mental imprisonment. You are not inferior. You have what it takes. Don't give up on yourself because no one has seen it in you. Even Walt Disney was once fired by a newspaper for lack of creativity. It happened to many successful people before they became well known. It's called 'life' and it's not personal. So don't take it too personally, just maintain your resolve to persevere till you succeed.

Treat everyone with dignity because everyone has potential. How do you want other people to treat you? Treat others that way. The rule of thumb is, *Do unto others as you would like them to do unto you.* R. H. Schuller says, "People who belittle people will be little people."

Jesus Chose the Most Unlikely Men

If any of us were in the position of Jesus, and were faced with the task of choosing leaders with whom to shape the world and carry out the divine task of redemption assigned by the Father, we would most certainly have combed every city and put up impressive adverts for the brightest minds around, with the best education and impressive track records to do the job. But the Lord Jesus chose for his disciples the most unlikely men. He chose laymen, rather than men from the religious hierarchy. He chose men from humble backgrounds with little formal education. His choice of fishermen rather than socialites would offend the sense of rationality of today's intellectuals. His assessment of leadership potential tended to cut right across popular opinion and the custom of that day. What about our own opinions? Who would have chosen such an unprepossessing group of untrained and uninfluential men as the apostles for a task with worldwide implications?

We certainly would have aimed to include in our group a prominent celebrity cum socialite, a renowned and influential member of the clergy, a university professor, a few PhDs, a successful businessman, a prominent statesman, and certainly, in this era where equality for women has become a popular chant, a woman of substance. But Jesus chose none of these.

For the class of men whom he chose, it would hardly be too much to say that no one but he would have discerned in that group of men the potential that gradually emerged as a result of their years of training under his able hands; for they soon displayed remarkable flair and proved to be an elite corps.

One remarkable quality stands out prominently in Christ: He does not judge by appearance, or by some external criteria. He is skilful with the use of His 'endoscope'. He looks as He should do because He not only looks *at* people, but *into* them as well. He sees beyond the skin colour, the social standing and all the other trivial externalities. He sees the hidden self, the real self and the inbuilt potential just waiting to be given a chance to explode. He looks beyond the present and sees what people have the potential to become, rather than just what they are now. His choice of men again brings to mind the truism of the saying by Goethe, "Look at a man the way that he is, and he only becomes worse. But look at him as if he were what he could be, then he becomes what he should be."

The Triumph of Jesse Owens

In what has been hailed as the greatest Olympic moment of all times, a 22-year-old Ohio State sophomore by the name of Jesse Owens took on the vaunted athletes of Adolf Hitler's racist Germany and demolished them, one by one, in four major track and field events. Adding insult to injury, the fleet-footed American accomplished his history-making feats on Hitler's own turf, the Olympic Stadium in the Nazi capital of Berlin, and with the dictator himself looking on.

At the opening ceremony, Hitler had refused to shake hands with Owens, bypassing him because he was black. No surprise. But in an ironic twist, the stadium, which Hitler had especially built as a world forum for the showcasing of his nation's athletic supremacy, became the stage for a black superman's triumph.

In an electrifying 100-meter dash, Owens tied the world record of 10.3 seconds, relegating his black team-mate Ralph Metcalfe to second place. In the 200-meter event, he defeated another fellow-American, Matthew Robinson, in 20.7 seconds. In the broad jump, Owens soared to a distance of 26 feet, $5^{5/16}$ inches, thereby defeating Germany's favourite Lutz Long and becoming the first Olympian to reach and surpass the 26-foot mark. Finally as a lead-off man in the 400-meter relay event, he helped his teammates to victory and himself to his fourth and final gold medal. Commenting about these events, a short paragraph in one edition of EBONY magazine reads:

Forgetting their racist dictator and his racist doctrines for a moment, thousands of German sports fans cheered ecstatically as a beaming Owens, who suddenly had emerged as the undisputed hero of the 1936 Olympic Games, again and again ascended the victor's stand to receive his unprecedented four medals.[11]

Jesse Owens' outstanding athletic accomplishment at the 1936 Olympic Games in Germany has been hailed as a triumph of decency over tyranny and bigotry.

My Mom's Going to Hear Me Play Someday

In recent times, I have been sent quite a few stories from friends by e-mail. Most of them were actual events, while others were made up. I consider it appropriate at this point to share with you one of the true stories that was sent to me by e-mail. I'd like you to hear it from Mildred herself, in her own words:

At the prodding of my friends, I am writing this story. My name is Mildred Hondorf. I am a former elementary school music teacher from Des Moines, Iowa.

I've always supplemented my income by teaching piano lessons – something I've done for 30 years. Over the years I found that children have many levels of musical ability. I've never had the pleasure of having a protégé though I have taught some talented students.

However I've also had my share of what I call 'musically challenged' pupils. One such student was Robby. Robby was 11 years old when his mother (a single mom) dropped him off for his first piano lesson. I prefer that students (especially boys) begin at an earlier age, which I explained to Robby.

But Robby said that it had always been his mother's dream to hear him play the piano. So I took him as a student. Well, Robby began with his piano lessons and from the beginning I thought it was a hopeless endeavour. As much as Robby tried, he lacked the sense of tone and basic rhythm needed to excel.

But he dutifully reviewed his scales and some elementary pieces that I require all my students to learn. Over the months he tried and tried while I listened and cringed and tried to encourage him. At the end of each weekly lesson he'd always say, "My mom's going to hear me play someday".

But it seemed hopeless. He just did not have any inborn ability. I only knew his mother from a distance as she dropped Robby off or waited in her car to pick him up. She always waved and smiled but never stopped in. Then one day Robby stopped coming to our lessons. I thought about calling him but assumed, because of his lack of ability, that he had decided to pursue something else. I also was glad that he stopped coming. He was a bad advertisement for my teaching!

Several weeks later, I mailed to the students' homes a flyer on the upcoming recital. To my surprise Robby (who received a flyer) asked me if he could be in the recital. I told him that the recital was for current pupils and because he had dropped, out he really did not qualify.

He said that his mom had been sick and unable to take him to piano lessons, but he was still practising.

"Miss Hondorf...I've just got to play!" he insisted. I don't know what led me to allow him to play in the recital. Maybe it was his persistence, or maybe it was something inside of me saying that it would be all right.

The night for the recital came. The high school gymnasium was packed with parents, friends and relatives. I put Robby up last in the programme before I was to come up and thank all the students and play a finishing piece. I thought that any damage he would do would come at the end of the program and I could always salvage his poor performance through my 'curtain closer'.

Well, the recital went off without a hitch. The students had been practising and it showed.

Then Robby came up on stage. His clothes were wrinkled and his hair looked like he had run an eggbeater through it.

"Why didn't he dress up like the other students?" I thought. "Why didn't his mother at least make him comb his hair for this special night?"

Robby pulled out the piano bench and he began. I was surprised when he announced that he had chosen Mozart's Concerto #21 in C Major. I was not prepared for what I heard next. His fingers were light on the keys, they even danced nimbly on the ivories. He went from pianissimo to fortissimo...from allegro to virtuoso. His suspended chords that Mozart demands were magnificent! Never had I heard Mozart played so well by people his age.

After six and a half minutes, he ended in a grand crescendo and everyone was on their feet in wild applause. Overcome and in tears, I ran up on stage and put my arms around Robby in joy.

'I've never heard you play like that Robby! How did you do it?'

Through the microphone, Robby explained to everyone:

'Well, Miss Hondorf...remember I told you my mom was sick? Well, actually she had cancer and passed away this morning. And well...she was born deaf, so tonight was the first time she ever heard me play. I wanted to make it special.'

There wasn't a dry eye in the house that evening. As the people from Social Services led Robby from the stage to be placed into foster care, I noticed that even their eyes were red and puffy and I thought to myself how much richer my life had been for taking Robby as my pupil.

No, I've never had a prodigy, but that night I became a protégé...of Robby's. He was the teacher and I was the pupil. For it is he that taught me the meaning of perseverance and love and believing in yourself, and maybe even taking a chance in someone and you don't know why.[12]

He Refused To Be Put Down

A young medical doctor once took his car to Tobago, a roadside mechanic, for repairs. This roadside mechanic was very good at what he did and had helped many people with their car problems. His satisfied clients were so happy with his services that most of them fondly called him Dr. Tobago. He actually didn't mind and was happy to be of service to his satisfied clients.

One fateful day, a medical doctor brought in his car to be fixed. As this young medical doctor sat in the mechanic workshop waiting for his car to be fixed, he couldn't help noticing how everyone was so crazy about this so-called 'Dr. Tobago.' Naturally, he became jealous. "This is misleading," he thought to himself. "I can't just sit here and let every Tom, Dick and Dhlamini call himself a doctor. Just because this ordinary roadside mechanic fixes cars doesn't give him the right to call himself a doctor." He argued aloud. "I think someone needs to put him where he belongs." Then all of a sudden, as if pulled off the shaky old bench he'd been impatiently sitting on by some strange force, he walked up to this 'Dr Tobago' to confront him and "get some answers."

"Tell me," he said, "why do you allow these people to keep calling you a doctor? That's very misleading. You are just a roadside mechanic and nothing more; can you make that very clear to them? It took real medical doctors like us several years of hard work and rigorous studies to earn this title. So you can't just sit in your mechanic workshop with no formal education and allow people to call you a doctor."

Dr. Tobago was a bit startled as he looked up from his work. Then, smiling calmly and putting his tools down, he looked at the young doctor and said, "I have no apologies for what my clients call me. I am good at what I do and they know it. You may have spent a few years in your medical school; I spent most of my life in apprenticeship learning what I do, that's why I do it so well. You probably work in someone's clinic; I am my own boss with many people working for me. My workshop is my clinic, and my apprentices are my nurses. I owe you no apologies for what people choose to call me. Besides, if you are as smart as you claim to be, why do you come to me to fix your car?"

Hmm! Tobago certainly took no prisoners. He held his ground and put this condescending doctor back in his place.

Consider again the following words from Job 12:3a (Amp):

But I have intelligence and understanding as well as you; I am not inferior to you."

POINTS TO PONDER

- The person you look down upon today and write off as unimportant, unintelligent, or incapable may end up becoming your boss tomorrow.

- Countless numbers of artists and actors who are very successful today were first turned down for lack of talent during their first auditions.

- Never again should you allow anyone to talk you into a state of perpetual mental imprisonment. You are not inferior. You have what it takes.

- The rule of thumb is, do unto others as you would like them to do unto you.

- Jesus looks beyond the present and sees what people have the potential to become, rather than what they are now.

> *Give me the ability to see good things in unexpected places and talents in unexpected people, and give me, O Lord, the grace to tell them so.*
> (From a 17th century nun's prayer)

APPLICATION ACTIVITIES

1. As you look back in your life, what important struggles in terms of any form of inferiority complex are you having, or have you had to deal with?

    (a) ....

    (b) ....

    (c) ....

2. What key concepts, stories or illustrations from this book can you recommend to someone who is still struggling with inferiority complex?

    (a) ....

    (b) ....

    (c) ....

Chapter Seven
YOUR RIGHT TO SUCCESS

Success means a person is reaching the maximum potential available to him at any given moment.
Ted Engstrom

Different people have different ideas of success. If you go on the street and interview ten different people on their idea of success, you will probably get ten different answers.

To some, success means reaching a top position in their place of work; to others, it is attaining their political ambitions; other people measure success by their professional titles, the size of their bank balance, the kind of houses they live in, their fame and popularity, the size of the crowd they pull when they perform on stage, or the kind and number of expensive cars they own.

So, to different people success means different things.

What is your idea of success?

To Abraham Lincoln, success could have meant achieving his goal of becoming the president of the United States of America after a life punctuated by repeated failures and painful defeats.

To Thomas A. Edison, success may have been inventing the incandescent light bulb after performing ten thousand unsuccessful experiments using different materials, including a human hair.

To David Livingstone, the Scottish pioneer missionary and explorer of Africa, success probably meant travelling thousands of miles through boisterous waves, daring mountains and thick jungles laden with man-eaters and savage tribes to discover what was then known as 'The Dark Continent', then giving his knowledge to the whole world.

To Robert H. Schuller, success may mean conquering financial handicap and capturing his dream of building and preaching in a glass house, the Crystal Cathedral, after preaching under the open sky every Sunday – summer, winter, spring and autumn – for six years.

To Dr. David Yonggi Cho of South Korea, success probably is raising and pastoring the largest single church in the world of over 800,000 members.

To Nelson Mandela of South Africa (fondly known as Madiba), success could have meant surviving a life sentence for high treason, and after spending 27 years in jail for his opposition to the apartheid regime, becoming the first black president of South Africa after an all-race, multiparty election.

A student's dream of success might be winning a scholarship to pursue his dream career abroad, or that golden moment when he receives his university degree.

A clinician's dream of success could be owning a chain of clinics in the city.

A driver may feel successful if he has a record of driving for thirty years without a single accident.

What is your idea of success?

To Jesus Christ of Nazareth, success means something that very few people would consider as such. To him success means offering up his life to carry the burden of sin for the whole world. He did not come to the world to be rich and famous, nor did he come to own a chain of successful corporations, or to be a successful investor in prime real estate. No, he had one mission on earth. That mission was his purpose, his passion and his priority. That mission defined and inspired everything he did on earth. His mission was to give his life to save the world. Although he lived for only thirty-three years and had only three years of active ministry, his life was a phenomenal success because he fulfilled his mission here on earth. Therefore, while hanging on the cross where he bore the burden of sin for the whole world, he exclaimed in his dying breath, "It is finished!" (John 19:30). Knowing and accomplishing his mission on earth – that is success.

The question, therefore, is not how long you lived, but how far you came in fulfilling your purpose for living.

So again…what is your idea of success?

- Getting a better job?
- Passing a difficult examination or interview?
- Enjoying good physical and mental health?
- Having a baby after many years of fruitless trials?
- Moving into your new home?
- Reaching and maintaining your target weight?
- Buying your first car?

Whatever your thoughts are about success, success is your God-given right, not a privilege. It is God's desire for you to prosper and succeed in all you do.

Beloved, I pray that you may prosper in all things and be in health, just as your soul prospers. (3 John verse 2 NKJV)

God has built within you all it takes to succeed. You have a right to it and can develop all that success potential within you.

You can –

- Live a successful and fruitful life.
- Make your dreams come true.
- Live above ruts and mediocrity.
- Achieve your goals and aspirations.
- Reach your maximum potential and be all God created you to be.

> *Success is discovering, developing and utilizing your God-given potential to be all that God created you to be.*

The Choice Is Yours

Whether you succeed or not, the choice is yours. The key to your success in life lies within yourself. There it remains in the personality of every individual waiting to be activated. It is latent in all human beings and will remain latent until it is realised and activated. This is partly the reason why sometimes you come across a person of obvious ability who is not living at a level of creativity that his aptitudes indicate he should attain. Obviously, the power of one's potential is more strongly seen in some people than in others. Those in whom that potential is seen are those who have learnt to draw from it to power their lives to success because they recognise their right to succeed.

Why do many potential geniuses pass through life without aim or purpose and consequently end up failures, while others make a great success out of every step they take? What is responsible for this difference?

On the one hand, you see a young man walking graciously down a city street with a lot of confidence in his eyes, an almost tangible aura of health and vitality about him and a sense of purpose in his stride, and on the other, you come upon some unfortunate derelict slumped against a wall, head sunk on chest, eyes staring vacantly into space, and idle hands folded away to waste, the whole scene presenting before you a picture of a helpless deaf-mute sunk in the quicksand of despondency. What is responsible for this difference?

To a very large extent, I am persuaded that the difference between these individuals lies in the extent to which they have been able to discover themselves, and refine and utilise their God-given potential. The good Lord was never partial in creation. He never made any group of persons to be more special or more endowed than others. Everyone was equally endowed. He made everything and everyone for a purpose. Success lies in the degree of your awareness of your purpose, and the extent to which you are accomplishing God's purpose for your life using the gifts and talents he has given you.

Your right to succeed is not negotiable. People end up as failures because they failed to follow God's plan in using God's resources in God's own way to walk in their God-ordained path to success.

Jeremiah 29:11 says, *For I know the plans I have for you, says the Lord. They are plans for good and not for evil, to give you a future and a hope.*

There is the story of a man called Jabez in the book of 1 Chronicles 4:9-10. When he was born, his mother chose to call him that name which means, 'son of sorrow,' because, in her own words, "I bare him with sorrow."

Jabez, a man whose name spelt what the rest of his life would look like – sorrow, pain, failure, and frustration – lived with this negative prophecy upon his life and future as he grew up. However, one day he discovered that the truth about one's right to succeed that we are discussing in the pages of this book was also applicable to him. He looked through his 'endoscope' and saw in himself potential for a happy and successful life, the very opposite of what his name meant. He saw in himself a man who was blessed, prosperous and happy, a man *honourable above his brothers*. With this new frame of mind and a very positive attitude, he went back to God and prayed what is today known as the classical 'Prayer of Jabez' that changed not only his life and future for good, but also the lives of thousands of people around the world who have prayed this same prayer:

"Oh, that You would bless me indeed, and enlarge my territory, that Your hand would be with me, and that You would keep me from evil, that I may not cause pain!" (1 Chronicles 4:10 NKJV*)*

He recognised his right to succeed, and he stripped his mind of every negative, defeatist image slammed on him from birth. Then he took his case file to the good Lord for review, and that was the turning point in his life. As the story goes, his request was granted by the Lord.

Andrew Was Down But Not Out

For Andrew, a young man whose dream was to become a business owner and entrepreneur, the future appeared bleak and hopeless. A thick cloud of darkness seemed to cover every ray of hope in his path as he took me through the snaky corridors of his difficult life. By the time I was counselling with him, Andrew had already been frustrated out of the one bedroom apartment where he was living with his mum, step-father, sibling and half-brothers. From the time he lost his father as a child, he had been struggling through life with very little or no support from his mum, step-father, or anyone. Due to lack of financial and moral support and encouragement, he passed out with very poor grades in his School Certificate exams. Things worsened when no one seemed to like his presence in the house anymore and he was seen more as a liability. Nothing he did was appreciated, and when things became unbearable for him, he left the house in frustration and left no clue as to where he was going. He decided to go and stay with a friend who had agreed to accommodate him to start life afresh. There, he scratched through life for survival and finally managed to get himself a poorly paid shift job with a shoe manufacturing company.

It was while on a visit to this friend that he was staying with, whom I also happened to know, that I stumbled across this young fellow. As I sat down with him and listened to his unhappy story, full of pain and sorrow, I recalled the story of Jabez and the prayer that changed his life forever.

After talking with Andrew for a while about his self-worth and his God-given success potential, something in him woke up; his face suddenly beamed with hope and he began to realise for the first time in his life that he had what it takes to succeed, that being down does not mean being out, that he could still pick up his life and make something worthwhile out of it. He suddenly realised that he didn't need to live a mediocre life of pain, regrets and sorrow if he didn't want to. So Andrew quickly rebuilt confidence in himself and in God's ability to restructure his life. As he gathered his shattered pieces of self-esteem together, he decided to change his frame of mind and put on a healthy mental attitude. His determination and new-found faith drove him to prompt action. Andrew realised during that brief encounter that he would never be what he ought to be, until he was doing what he ought to be doing. Right then and there, he knew what he had to do. He was determined to do it or die trying. Andrew wasted no time. Within a few days, he arranged for a private teacher to prepare him for the General Certificate of Education (GCE) examination because his new resolve was to go back to school, make the grades and head straight for a university degree. Thereafter, he would pursue his dream of becoming a business owner and entrepreneur. He would settle for nothing less because he now realised that he too, like anyone else, had the right to succeed.

Many years have passed since then. So I decided to check on Andrew again recently. I called up the same friend through whom I had met Andrew to find out how he had fared since my last encounter with him. He told me that Andrew had not looked back since that encounter. He had saved up some money, gone back to school, and had completed his education. Thereafter, he went into business, working for himself as a business owner and entrepreneur. Today Andrew owns and runs a successful dry cleaning business in Lagos. What's more, Andrew is married to a beautiful wife, and together, they have two beautiful kids. His life's story has become a true epitome of the saying that 'When life hands you a lemon, make lemonade.'

Severe Physical Handicaps Could Not Stop Her

Once you recognise your right to succeed, nothing but yourself can stop you – not even a physical handicap. The incredible Helen Keller is an outstanding example of a person who conquered physical handicaps and shot herself to glory and fame because she too recognised her right to succeed. Her life's story is a challenge as well as a rebuke to those who have confined themselves to a mental wheelchair by accepting defeat in believing that the door of success and achievement has been slammed against them permanently because of some physical handicap.

When she was only 19 months old, Helen Adams Keller lost both sight and hearing from a serious illness. She was thus unable to learn to speak, and was entirely shut off from the world. Despite these handicaps, the blind, deaf and dumb Keller triumphed and achieved world fame as a lecturer and author, and gained world recognition for her aid to the handicapped.

How did she do it?

When Helen was 7, Miss Anne Sullivan, of the Perkins Institute of the Blind, came to live with her. Miss Sullivan taught her to read by Braille and to write using a special typewriter. Later Helen was taught to speak. Helen Keller made many lecture tours and wrote several books. She brought a message of courage to the disabled everywhere. This indomitable spirit is still available for all who desire it. Let but the jaw set in resolve and the mind say *I will!* And all things are possible.

> *They conquer who think they can.*
> John Dryden

A man named Jack Clemo faced deafness, blindness, financial hardship, failure to get a wife, and rejection of his manuscripts. But later in life he won the Atlantic prize for his first novel, married at the age of 52 and became known as one of Britain's great poets.

Being crippled did not stop Shakespeare from writing the world's finest plays. Being blind did not stop John Milton from writing England's greatest poem, *Paradise Lost*. Being stone deaf did not stop Ludwig van Beethoven from composing some of the most beautiful pieces of music ever written.

History is full of people who accomplished great things in spite of serious handicaps. Alexander the Great was a hunchback. Handel's right hand was paralysed when he composed his great work *The Hallelujah Chorus*. Thomas Edison was deaf when he invented the phonograph. You may say, "Couldn't these people have accomplished so much more if they hadn't been handicapped?" Maybe. Maybe not.

There is an ancient account of a great soldier who had a deadly disease that could kill him at any time. Because he was expecting to die at any moment, when he was sent to the war front, he became completely fearless in battle. He fought gallantly because he had nothing to lose. He was extremely brave and fought so fearlessly that his General, noticing his bravery, admired him.

The army General thought of finding a way to cure the soldier by sending him to the best treatment centre available. The soldier was treated and his affliction removed.

Returning from medical treatment, the once valiant soldier did not want to go back to the battlefield. He was now afraid to die. His good health and comfort destroyed his will to fight, his bravery and courage, and thus, his usefulness as a soldier.

So often, physical handicap brings out the best in people and impels them to fight against the odds and achieve heights of accomplishment that they otherwise would not have aimed for. You can't change what happened to you, but you can change what you do about it. It was the American author and motivational speaker, Jim Rohn, who said:

> *Don't wish it was easy; wish you were better.*
> *Don't wish for less problems; wish for more skills.*
> *Don't wish for less challenge; wish for more wisdom.*

Difficulties make us better, problems make us tougher, and it is the challenges we face that make us stronger. When you fall into a river full of crocodiles, don't fight them. You are not going to win. Rather make them your friends and learn to swim with them. That is the secret of survival.

Lack of Education Is No Excuse

Many people have grown to believe the error that only the well-educated and those who make the best grades in school can have real success and breakthrough in life. Nothing could be further from the truth. A good education is good; good grades in school are also good, but a lack of them does not strip you of your right to succeed. We need not go too far in history to draw up splendid examples of uneducated men and women, and those labelled 'uneducable dunces' who made their mark in the arena of greatness and achievement.

Thomas Alva Edison, the 'electric wizard' who believed that genius is about 2% inspiration and 98% perspiration is generally considered the greatest inventor in history because of the effect his inventions have had on our lives. But this same man was considered a dunce by his teacher and had only three months of formal education. As a schoolboy, Edison was sent home with a note from his teacher saying that he could not learn, that he could not think, and that he was stupid. Yet this remarkable man did not put himself down, or see himself as a dunce who was fit only to take orders from well-schooled superiors. Edison accepted the fact that there was a power in existence bigger than himself, and he learnt to work in complete harmony with that power. Thus, with God's help, he broke out from the rut and revolutionised the world with his inventions. The incandescent lamp, phonograph and countless other inventions are credited to his inventive ingenuity.

Another genius, Albert Einstein, was written off as uneducable by his teacher, and was considered a slow learner and retarded. But he knew he had potential and was determined to prove it by putting it to use. He proved his teacher wrong as he became one of the greatest scientists the world ever had. His theory of relativity, by which he laid the basis for the application of atomic energy and set forth new ideas of time, space, mass motion, and gravitation, was considered one of the greatest intellectual achievements in history. Thus, he inscribed his name boldly in the minds of scientists through many generations.

Countless other highly successful men and women have had a limited education. Yet, they made a mark in their various fields of calling. Now this is by no means a celebration of mediocrity, or an endorsement of illiteracy. On the contrary, it is a clear reminder that failure in school and a deficiency in academic aptitude does not necessarily equate to failure in life.

Joseph, the son of Jacob in the Bible, had neither a degree in political science nor a paper qualification of any sort. All he had with him was his integrity and his little gift of interpretation of dreams. He developed this God-given gift and learnt to use it at the right time, and that shot him to an enviable position of prominence so that he became a great ruler in Egypt, second only to Pharaoh.

Few apostles in the New Testament like Paul had some education. Great disciples of Jesus like Peter, James and John were fishermen. They had no formal education. But in their days, men testified that they "turned the world upside down" (Acts 17:6).

Recognise and appreciate the person God has made you to be. See yourself as a winner, not a loser. Look at yourself from a healthy biblical perspective. Approach life differently – with a positive mental attitude. Be grateful for what you have and stop making comparisons or lamenting your inadequacies. Success is within your reach. Your life matters to God; don't throw it away. Never put yourself down. You have more abilities than you can imagine.

Do not be comfortable in the crowd. Find your path for success and walk in it with courage and determination, and sooner than you think, it will slope down to your gold mine. It may not be easy, but it will be worth it in the end. Always look for an opportunity to stand out. ***The world always stands aside and lets the man pass who knows where he is going.***

Whatever your goals, they are not unattainable; whatever your dreams, they are not unachievable; whatever your mountains, they are not insurmountable. Ask for it. Go for it. Believe you can. ***All things are possible to him who believes.***

If you think it, you can do it.
If you dream it, you can become it.
Anonymous

The only person who can stop you from becoming what God wants you to be is YOU!

Reaffirm to yourself: "I am somebody. I am a child of God. They may call me illiterate or untutored; I may be crippled or deformed; I may be deaf and dumb or blind, but I am somebody. I have a God-given right to succeed, and God helping me, I will surely make it!"

In *The Westminster Collection of Christian Quotations,* the editor, Martin H. Manser, credited the following quotation to Ted W. Engstrom:

Cripple a man, and you have Sir Walter Scott; lock him in prison and you have John Bunyan; bury him in the snow of Valley Forge and you have George Washington; raise him in poverty and you have Abraham Lincoln; strike him down with infantile paralysis and he becomes Franklin Delano Roosevelt; burn him so severely that doctors say he will never walk again and you have Glen Cunningham, who set the world's record in 1934 for the one-minute mile; deafen him and you'll have Ludwig Van Beethoven; call him a slow learner, retarded, and write him off as uneducable and you have Albert Einstein.[13]

Dispel, repel, repudiate the assumption that because you are from a poor family with severe limitations you must never dream of success. The winners of this world are not those who easily succumb to the fake threats of life or the conditional shadows of fate. They are the ones who courageously fight the battles of life in the face of financial hardship, educational deprivation, and lack of moral hinges from doubting Thomases. God so often picks the unknown, the unheralded, and the uncelebrated to do the impossible. He uses the foolish things of the world to confound the wise. Jesus was born in poverty, raised in obscurity, yet since His time the world has never known a greater leader, teacher, miracle worker...the list goes on. You had a more honourable birth than he, and probably a more dignified background. So, there is no alibi to waive your lack of accomplishment of God's success plan for your life.

With the following words of educator Horace Mann, I throw a challenge to you:

Be ashamed to die until you have
won some victory for humanity.
Horace *Mann*

POINTS TO PONDER

- Success is your God-given right and not a privilege. You have within your reach all it takes to succeed.
- Success is discovering, developing, and utilising your God-given potential to be all that God created you to be.
- The key to your success in life lies within yourself.
- The question, therefore, is not how long you lived, but how far you came in fulfilling your purpose for living.
- Poor school grades, lack of formal education, or a physical handicap does not strip you of your right to succeed.
- The world will always stand aside and let you pass if you know where you are going.
- Whatever your goals, they are not unattainable; whatever your dreams, they are not unachievable; whatever your mountains, they are not insurmountable. All things are possible to them who believe.
- If you think it, you can do it; if you dream it, you can become it.
- Be ashamed to die until you have won some victory for humanity.

> *You have not done enough,*
> *you have never done enough,*
> *so long as it is still possible that*
> *you have something to contribute.*
> Dag Hammerskjold

APPLICATION ACTIVITIES

1. What excuses have you been using for your state of non-achievement?

- ☐ Poor family background.
- ☐ Lack of opportunities.
- ☐ Wrong environment.
- ☐ Lack of moral and financial support.
- ☐ Lack of education.
- ☐ Wrong advice / lack of good advice.
- ☐ Bad personal decisions and choices.
- ☐ Being in the wrong company (bad friends, losers).
- ☐ Age disadvantage (I am too old / too young).
- ☐ Others (list them)..

2. For every point you checked, what are you going to do about it and when? (Be as clear and as specific as possible).

Chapter Eight

MAKE A PLAN FOR YOUR SUCCESS

The heights by great men reached and kept
Were not attained by sudden flight;
But they, while their companions slept
Were toiling upward in the night.
Author Unknown

Every successful endeavour in life is a product of good planning and good thinking. Every ship cruising the Indian Ocean, every aircraft that Boeing has ever built, every skyscraper outlining the skylines of New York, every successful mission to space, and every bridge across the Lagos lagoon is a product of good planning and good thinking. No great accomplishment is a product of chance. Even winning the lottery requires buying a ticket.

People may fail by accident, but rarely does anyone stumble into success by accident. To expect to succeed by accident would be a huge gamble. Every success has a plan which is carefully executed to achieve desired results. If you plan to succeed, you will succeed with your plans. But if you fail to plan, you are planning to fail because you have failed to observe one of the cardinal laws of success.

For All Success There Is a Plan

- For every successful business, there is a business plan that provides direction, ensures viability, determines utility and distribution of resources, projects and promotes profitability, eliminates guesswork, and minimises the risk of failure.
- For every successful marriage, there is a formula – strong convictions, a solid foundation of love and mutual respect, lasting commitment and trust, good planning, and carefully set long-range goals that transcend just the wedding day.

- For every successful corporation, there is a vision and mission statement that defines existence, ensures focus, determines activities, propels growth and productivity, and gauges success.
- For every successful battle, there is a battle plan that ensures cohesion and coordination, maximises resources, minimises surprises, eliminates guesswork and increases the chance of victory.
- For every successful building project, there is a building plan, a blueprint, an architectural design that converts concepts into pictures, guides the builders, sets dimensions, defines the boundaries, determines resources, and ensures accuracy, quality, and standards.

For all success, there is a price. For all success, there is also a plan, a strategy or a formula. Success doesn't just happen by chance; something or someone makes it happen by consciously executing a carefully worked out plan or strategy. You need no strategy or plan to fail, but you cannot succeed without a conscious, deliberate strategy or plan.

To become great in life, your plan does not always have to begin and end with you. Sometimes your plan has to be a long-range plan that will outlive you. That is because, what you do for yourself, you take to the grave with you, but what you do for others, you leave behind after you are gone. When your success plan includes and becomes a road map for future generations, then you will have succeeded in building a bridge of hope and contributed to posterity something for which you will be remembered and celebrated long after you have left this planet.

To put this into perspective, consider the following poem by Will Allen Dromgoole:[14]

THE BRIDGE BUILDER

An old man, going a lone highway,
Came, at the evening, cold and grey,
To a chasm, vast, and deep, and wide,
Through which was flowing a sullen tide.

The old man crossed in the twilight dim;
The sullen stream had no fears for him;
But he turned, when safe on the other side
And built a bridge to span the tide.

"Old man," said a fellow pilgrim, near,
"You are wasting strength with building here;
Your journey will end with the ending day;
You never again must pass this way;
You have crossed the chasm, deep and wide –
Why build you a bridge at the eventide?"

The builder lifted his old grey head:
"Good friend, in the path I have come," he said,
"There followeth after me today,
A youth, whose feet must pass this way.

This chasm, that has been naught to me,
To that fair-haired youth may a pitfall be.
He, too, must cross in the twilight dim;
Good friend, I am building the bridge for him."

Following this old man's example, your success plan must include a long-range plan which takes into account future generations, so that it continues to succeed long after you have contributed your part and exited this dimension. Otherwise, if there is no continuity, if there is no generational transfer, if you take with you to the grave your success, you would have lived and died a successful failure, and that would be a great tragedy.

For All Success, There Is a Price

The price of greatness is the same as the price of success. Winston Churchill said, *"The price of greatness is responsibility."* If this is true, and I believe that it is, then the price of success is also responsibility. When responsible actions that constitute a success formula are taken, success becomes inevitable.

What then is responsibility?

Dr. Myles Monroe defines responsibility as the *"ability to respond to your God-given ability."* The ability to recognise your ability is a rare gift, but the ability to respond to your ability is even rarer. That is probably why so many are still far from the threshold of greatness.

Everyone is created to be great in some way. Accepted. But the degree to which you attain greatness in your God-chosen area is largely determined by the degree to which you have accepted responsibility in that area. You cannot run away from, or neglect your abilities in any area and expect to become great by the same.

To all success, there is a price. The price you pay for success is not always only for yourself, but it could also be for the freedom, liberation, and upliftment of others. For example, Mahatma Gandhi booked his ticket on the flight to greatness through his personal sacrifice and non-violent resistance to free his people from tyranny and injustice. Also, for the freedom of others, Nelson Mandela earned his place in the books of history, not just for what he did for himself, but more so for what he did for millions of black South Africans who suffered oppression under the repressive white apartheid regime. For the freedom of his people, Nelson Mandela gave up his own freedom and spent 27 years in prison so his people could be free. If success seems to come easy for you, if you appear to succeed without sacrifice, then it is probably because someone who went before you has already made the sacrifice or paid the price. In the same vein, if you sacrifice or pay a huge price and do not see success immediately, do not despair; you have also succeeded, but you've done so by successfully paving the way for someone who follows you to reap success from your sacrifice.

For All Success, There Is Responsibility

We have already established that there is a price for all success, and taking responsibility is part of the price you have to pay for your spot on the platform of greatness. Success in any endeavour in life cannot be achieved or maintained without responsibility. A man who bequeaths his wealth to his child stands the risk of losing everything in just a short time unless he first teaches his child to accept responsibility.

Here are some areas where a man must teach his child to take responsibility if he expects to leave a lasting legacy when he is gone:

1. *Attitude*

    You cannot have the attitude of mediocrity and hope to walk on the streets of greatness. It is your attitude towards life that determines life's attitude towards you. Your attitude in life will always determine how far you can go and how great you can become. If you radiate a positive attitude of confidence, of wellbeing, and of a person who knows where he is going, the world will stand aside and let you through, and positive things will begin to happen in your life. On the other hand, if you go through life feeling defeated, walking around looking like a suspect not a prospect – with pants down and tattoos in all sorts of places – doors will appear to close each time you show up, and life will address you as you are dressed. So develop the attitude now that there are more reasons why you should succeed, why you deserve to be recognised, and why you should stand up and be counted with the best, and life will respond and say "Amen!"

2.   *Vision and dreams*

Vision is the ability to see things, not as they are, but as they could become. Vision is foresight, looking ahead and seeing that which is not presently visible. Your vision and dreams are closely related. Your dreams are your aspirations, what you hope to achieve or become in future. You see it in your mind even before you become it. What you constantly visualise yourself to be is what you are likely to become. What you dream about is what you think about; what you think about is what you are likely to become. That's why they say, "If you can dream it, you can achieve it." The size of your dream will determine how big a person you will be; and the size of your vision will determine how far ahead you can go. He who does not see ahead will remain behind.

3.   *Knowledge*

This is the acquisition of information concerning a given field of endeavour. There are four things you must know if you are to get to the top:

a) Know who you are. Do you know who God says you are, or do you only know who other people have made you believe you are? Are you easily swayed, or are you resolute and firm? Are you easily distracted or are you determined and focused? Self-knowledge is the ability to know yourself, your abilities and limitations, what you can or cannot do, when to go for it and when to stop and seek help. You can know yourself by doing a thorough self-analysis, and by really finding out all that God says about you in His Word.

b) Know what you have. You must know your gifts, your talents, your abilities, your strengths, and your capabilities. If you know what you have on your inside, nothing on the outside can upset you. An African proverb says, *If there is no enemy within, the enemy outside can do me no harm.* Greater is He that is in you than he that is in the world. When you know that you have greatness in you, nothing you face will intimidate or move you. When you know that what lies behind you and what lies before you are tiny matters compared to what lies within you, then nothing around you can cause you to belittle yourself or sell yourself short.

c) Know where you are going. Where are you heading in life? Are you on your way to the top, or are you just going through life with no clear objective, but hope that one day, somehow, you will end up at the top? If you don't have any clearly stated destination, you could end up anywhere, including in prison. Where you are right now is irrelevant so long as you know where you are going, you put a focus to it, and you take little baby steps every single day towards your desired destination.

d) Know what it takes to get there. If you know who you are, what you have, and where you are going, the next step is to know what it takes to get you to that position. This is now the time to go beyond dreaming, visualising, and just thinking and talking positively. It is time to go one important step further: make a definite plan and set specific goals for actualising those plans.

4. *Determination and persistence*

No one ever succeeds without determination and persistence. If you are determined to make it, to demand more from life, and to reach your goals, nothing can stop you – not even failure and temporary setbacks. That is why one of the surest ways to win is to be determined to succeed. It was the novelist David Ambrose who said, *If you have the will to win, you have achieved half your success; if you don't, you have achieved half your failure.* If you keep trying, you will eventually win, but if you stop trying, then you have chosen the slippery road to failure. Napoleon Hill agrees when he says, *The longer you walk in the right direction, the closer you are to success. Too many people give up when success is within their grasp. They leave it for someone else to capture.*[15] To succeed, you need to make plans and back those plans with persistence and resolve. Be determined to never, ever give up, even if you meet with setbacks, as you often will.

5. *Planning and goal setting*

All successful people are great strategists and planners. They always plan a few steps ahead, they are proactive and they plan for risks and contingencies. They are people who refuse to allow their environment or personal circumstances to define them. They free themselves from mental limitations and align their thoughts with those of Mark Caine who said, "The first step towards success is taken when you refuse to be a captive of the environment in which you first find yourself." All great men manage the future instead of allowing the future to manage them. They are not participants in the blame game, but they go out there and look for opportunities instead of sitting down and waiting for opportunities to come to them. As George Bernard Shaw put it, "People are always blaming their circumstances for what they are. I don't believe in circumstances. The people who get on in this world are people who get up and look for the circumstances they want, and if they can't find them, make them." Planning is a source of their confidence, direction, and strength. They accomplish their dreams by careful planning and goal setting. Goal setting is the vehicle that takes you from dreamland to reality land, from the realm of just dreaming to the realm of actualising your dreams and making them come true. Goal setting helps you to accomplish your vision and bring it to fruition. Without goal setting, your visions are reduced to wishful thinking, and your dreams degenerate into nightmares. A man without a dream is a drifter. If he has one but has no plan for bringing it to fruition, he is comparable to the proverbial drifter called Mr. Easy Life.

When asked where he was going, Mr. Easy Life replied, "I am going somewhere."

"When do you hope to get there?" he was asked.

"Sometime," he responded.

"And how do you hope to get there?"

"Emm, well, I will get there somehow," he replied hesitantly, looking confused and scratching his itchy bald head.

While Mr. Easy Life tries to figure out how to get "somewhere," if he ever decides at all, here are a few steps to help you set your goals and develop a road map to the land of greatness:

Goal Setting In Ten Steps

1. *Decide what you want to achieve.*

   What are your dreams? What are your aspirations? What do you want to achieve in life? The first step in goal setting is deciding what those goals are that you want to achieve. In making this decision, it is important that your goal is something you really want, not just something that sounds good. You can have goals for different areas of your life. For instance, your goals can be classified into categories such as:

   ✓ What you want to be (being):

   For example, "By the end of this year, I want to be a better husband and father who spends more time with my family and help with my kids' homework."

   ✓ What you plan to do (doing):

   For example, "I plan to free up enough time (about 5 hours a week) to mow the lawn, water the garden and take my family out for a picnic at least once every week."

   ✓ What you plan to own (owning):

   For example, "I plan to own a holiday home worth $100,000.00 by the beach near Richards Bay, a white Toyota SUV, and a Gypsy Caravan within the next three years."

   ✓ What you hope to accomplish (accomplishing):

For example, I plan to earn an MBA at Harvard and become a senior manager in my organisation within the next five years.

2. *Write down your goals.*
It is not enough to keep your well thought out goals in your mind. Your goals must be clearly written down so that you don't forget. That way, you also have something to look at to remind you and spur you on. Part of what you accomplish in writing down your goals is to create a set of instructions for your subconscious mind to carry out. Your goals could be framed around the following areas of your life to create a perfect balance:
- ✓ Physical/health goals
- ✓ Spiritual/ethical goals
- ✓ Career/financial goals
- ✓ Social/recreational goals
- ✓ Marital/family/relationship goals, and so on.

3. *Break your main goal into smaller sub-goals.*
Larger difficult goals should be broken down into a number of smaller manageable goals or sub-goals. That way, the main goal becomes less intimidating and easier to manage. Each of the sub-goals must constitute an important part of the main goal. By the time you achieve all your sub-goals, your main goal is already conquered.

4. *Organise your list into a plan.*
After setting your main goals and sub-goals, organise them in such a way that you are inspired to take action each time you look at them. Classify your goals into long-term and short-term goals. You could start at 20 years, then 10 years, then 5 years, then 3 years, then 1 year. You could set short-term goals for 9 months, then 6 months, then 3 months, and then 1 month. Goals could also be set weekly, daily, and even hourly, so that by doing

something every hour of every day to reach your goals, before long, your goals will be accomplished.

5. *Attach a target date to each goal and sub-goal.*
   This means that you decide and set a specific due deadline that you strive to beat. Estimate how long it will take for you to reach your goal. Then set a deadline. This deadline should be realistic – that is, not too short or too long. If you do not achieve your goal by the due date, don't be discouraged – just adjust the due date and get back to work. Be flexible enough to change due dates or even put a particular goal on hold should the need arise. But also be disciplined enough to avoid the trap of procrastination simply because you know that your due date can be moved.

6. *Make your goals and sub-goals SMART[16].*
   That means that for your goals and sub-goals to be good, they have to be:
   ✓ *Specific.*
   Your goals must not be vague, but clear and specific. For example, a goal such as "I want to be a millionaire" is very vague and will be difficult, if not impossible to achieve.
   ✓ *Measurable.*
   You must be able to tell when you have achieved your goals by making them measurable. The goal of a car salesman, for instance, could be to increase his car sales from 10 to 20 cars in one month. That goal is measurable and anyone can tell at the end of the month whether or not he achieved his goal.
   ✓ *Attainable.*
   Set goals that can be attained. They must not be too high, otherwise you get discouraged and frustrated along the way when you find no way of attaining them. They should not be too simple either, otherwise you find no satisfaction in conquering them. They must be challenging enough to keep

you motivated, and to give you a strong sense of satisfaction when you accomplish them.

✓ *Realistic.*

If your goals are not realistic, they cannot be accomplished. A 10-year-old boy whose goal is to become a commercial airline pilot by the time he is 15 is setting an unattainable goal that is bound to fail. This is because no sensible airline company in the world will entrust the lives and safety of their passengers in the hands of a 15-year-old boy no matter how well trained. He simply does not have the physical and emotional maturity to shoulder such responsibility.

✓ *Time-bound.*

The need to attach a deadline to your goals and sub-goals has already been discussed. Without deadlines, you reduce your goals and sub-goals into a mere wish list. It is, however, possible to have a goal such as "to be a person of honesty and integrity" that is on-going, sustained over time, and therefore never ending.

7. *List all the steps necessary to reach your goal.*

What steps are needed to take you to your desired destination? What resources do you need? What set of skills, training or knowledge are required? What personnel, techniques or methods will be needed to help you achieve your goals? What activities are required? What obstacles will you need to overcome? Put pen to paper and draw up a list for each case. That list gives you a clear picture of what you are up against. Analyse the list, rewrite it, and determine what needs to be done first – prioritise.

8. *Take action.*

Don't wait for things to happen – make them happen. Opportunities seldom come to those who wait; they are seized by those who are on the move, the go-getters. Little steps every day become great steps someday. Take that step today. Don't just sit around waiting for the elevator to success to come to you. It may never come. It could be out of order, so you'll have to use the stairs – one step at a time. You cannot become a big shot someday unless you start shooting today, because big shots are only small shots who kept on shooting. Start shooting NOW! Start small, start slowly, and keep it simple. But start! *Success is the sum of small efforts, repeated day-in and day-out,* says Robert Collier.

9. *Review your goals.*
    Constantly review your goals as you go along and as circumstances change. Check your progress daily. Re-strategize where necessary. Adjust deadlines as occasion warrants. Reward yourself and celebrate for every milestone achievement reached – every major goal conquered. That way, you stay motivated.

10. *Set new goals.*
    Robert H. Schuller said, "Fear not that you might fail…fear rather that you might never succeed if you never dare to try." As you come close to achieving your current goal, that is the time to start setting new goals. Life is about making progress, accomplishing, growing. The whole world is constantly on the move. If you stop growing, you start aging.

> *You must have long-range goals*
> *to keep you from being*
> *frustrated by short-term failures.*
> Charles C. Noble

If you follow the guidelines outlined in this chapter to make a plan for your success every day, you will be on your way to achieving unlimited success in every area of your life. You will also:

- ✓ Increase your self-confidence
- ✓ Improve your performance
- ✓ Accomplish more every day
- ✓ Suffer less from anxiety and stress
- ✓ Be more focused and purposeful in life
- ✓ Be better organised
- ✓ Be healthier and happier
- ✓ Be more determined and motivated to succeed

In conclusion, greatness in any endeavour in life requires vision. All great men have been men of vision. But vision in itself is not enough. The vision must be brought to fruition, not by sitting around and waiting for conditions to be perfect – they may never be – but by putting together a SMART and well thought-out plan that involves doing something small every single day to bring you closer to actualising your vision and dreams. If you set your daily goals well, and reach them, your monthly goals will automatically be reached. If your monthly goal is reached, then your yearly goal has to happen. And by hitting your yearly goals every year, then your life-long goal cannot but be reached. That way, with God's help, you take your destiny in your own hand and sculpt your future the way you want it to be. By planning your life creatively in this way, you lift yourself and your future onto the path of greatness.

POINTS TO PONDER

- Every successful endeavour in life is a product of good planning and good thinking.
- If you plan to succeed, you will succeed with your plans. But if you fail to plan, you are planning to fail because you have failed to observe one of the cardinal laws of success.
- You need no strategy or plan in order to fail, but you cannot succeed without a conscious effort to do so.
- When responsible actions that constitute a success formula are taken, success becomes inevitable.
- If you radiate a positive attitude of confidence, of wellbeing, and of a person who knows where he or she is going, the world will stand aside and let you pass, and positive things will begin to happen in your life.
- Don't just sit around waiting for the elevator to success to come to you. It may never come. It could be out of order, so you'll have to use the stairs – one step at a time.
- Develop the attitude now that there are numerous reasons why you should succeed, why you deserve to be recognised, and why you should stand up and be counted with the best, and life will respond and say "Amen!"

> *A blind man's world is bounded*
> *By the limits of his touch;*
> *An ignorant man's world*
> *By the limits of his knowledge;*
> *A great man's world by the limits*
> *Of his vision.*
> E. Paul Hovey

APPLICATION ACTIVITIES

1. Mention one important principle you've learned in this chapter that you can apply this coming week.
    Principle:………………………………………………………………...

2. Write down the name of one person with whom you can share and discuss what you have learned in this chapter. Also write down a date and time within the next week when you hope to contact and meet with this person for discussion.
    Name:……………………………………………………………
    Date:………………………………………………………..………
    Time:……………………………………………………………..

3. In readiness for this meeting, pick one of your most important dreams or aspirations, and formulate a detailed plan for its actualization during this meeting, using some of the SMART goal-setting techniques mentioned in this chapter.

4. What would it mean for you to achieve your goals and realise your dreams? What would the feeling be like for you? Write it down.

5. Here is your daily dose of 'Motivate': your motivational self-talk. Dosage: Three times daily for seven days:

    I can!
    I want to!!
    I will!!!
    I'm going to!!!!

Chapter Nine

YOU CAN HANDLE DEFEATS

Success is a continuum. At one end is what we call
failure; at the opposite end is success and satisfaction.
Success begins with failure and ends with accomplishments.
Seen this way, failure is an anticipated part of the success process.
Unknown

Have you been defeated?

Have you encountered problems?

Have you experienced failure or setbacks?

The problems you face, the defeats you suffer, and the setbacks you encounter can either defeat you or develop you, depending on how you respond to them.

Unfortunately, most people who meet with failure and temporary defeat often see it as something that is an absolute no-no. They fail to see how God wants to use temporary setbacks for good in their lives. They react foolishly and resent these temporary setbacks rather than considering what benefits they might bring. Success often comes out of failure, and no one who aspires to be great can totally avoid the risk of failure – ask any great man you know. Success is adopting the right attitude towards failure.

Failure and defeat are two undeniable facts of life. We have all been defeated here and there. We have all experienced failure at one time or the other. Great lessons of success are contained in every failure. Problems help us to learn to be patient, and patience develops strength of character. It was John Maxwell who posed the following challenge: *The question is not if you will have problems, but how you are going to deal with your problems.*[17]

No one was born with immunity to failure. But we can turn the handle of every failure to our advantage by making it a learning experience. Someone once said that, 'within the seed of every failure is the potential for a greater success.' The only way to succeed in life is to take risks – risks that involve the real possibility of failure. We must accept that the risk of failure is an inherent possibility that comes with every opportunity to succeed. As a matter of fact, unless you know how to fail, you will never really know how to succeed. This also means that you do not back down from an opportunity to succeed simply because there lies in it an equal opportunity to fail.

A man who competes in a race with nine other athletes does not back out because his chances of winning the race is only ten per cent. The fact that his chance of winning the race is only one in ten, and he has a ninety per cent chance of losing still does not stop an athlete from competing. The odds for a sperm cell to fertilise a female egg is about 40 million to one. Does that stop the sperm from trying? Not at all! There will always be competition, and the risk of failure will always, always, be there. But a wise athlete always thinks about the positives – his chances of winning, how to run in order to get to the finish line first, and the prize at stake – not on his chances of losing the race because of the high risk of failure. If there is no competition, then winning is no longer fun, the trophy will have no value, and all the thrills will be gone. The fact is, if the athlete does not join the race because of fierce competition and the high risk of failure, he can never win. There is no other way.

The right attitude to failure is very important for anyone who aspires to be great in any sphere of life. Every failure is a learning experience. With each failure, you are wiser and better off than when you started because you learn an important lesson that you wouldn't learn any other way. I was thinking about this subject when I wrote the following lines a few years ago:

Failure is a book that teaches on the best way to succeed.
Receive it with thankfulness;
Read it with hopefulness;
Analyse it with carefulness;
Apply it with faithfulness;

Pursue it with steadfastness,
and Nothing will stop you from reaching your goal.

So, I ask you:

How do you view failure and temporary setbacks?

What is your attitude towards the obstacles you face in life?

Do you allow them to become a source of discouragement or a key to new discoveries?

It is your attitude in life that determines your altitude in life. You can allow your setbacks to become stumbling blocks, or you can turn them into stepping stones for great comebacks. It's all in your attitude. According to William Arthur Ward, *Success is sometimes a series of failures held together by the strong strand of determination and persistence.*

Failure is not a fact. It's an opinion. What one man sees as failure, another man sees as opportunity. What one man sees as an impossibility, another sees as a mere challenge that needs to be broken down and tackled piece by piece.

Greatness in life consists, not only in having a good feeling about success, but also the right attitude towards failure. Many people have taken their own lives because of setbacks in life and failure to achieve their goals. If only they had held the right attitude towards failure, they would have known that our greatest glory is not in never failing, but in rising every time we fail. They would have also known that there is no failure except in no longer trying. They would also have known that failure is never final; it is only a lap in the marathon of success, a chapter in the book of achievement, and one of the ingredients in the recipe of greatness.

Greatness in life consists, not only
in having a good feeling about success,
but also the right attitude towards failure.

In dealing with the vicissitudes of life, Claire Rayner suggests a technique that she learnt from her grandmother, a phrase that is to be used at all times in your life:

When things are spectacularly dreadful; when things are absolutely appalling; when everything is superb and wonderful and marvellous and happy – say these words to yourself: "This too will pass." They will give you a sense of perspective and help you to make the most of what is good and to be stoical about what is bad.

The right attitude towards failure and temporary defeats is important as we ascend the steps to greatness. In his 1818 letter to James Hassey, it was John Keats who said, *I would sooner fail than not be among the greatest.* The journey to be among the greatest is a long and arduous journey filled with many pitfalls. That is why it is important to learn how to handle failure. Abraham Lincoln had many painful setbacks and defeats on his way to greatness. That did not stop him because he knew how not to let his setbacks stand in his way.

As we walk the path to greatness, here are some points, distilled from the wisdom of great men, which we need to note about failure in order to encourage us to not throw away opportunities because of the tight rope of failure that we have to walk to reach our goal:

- It is nobler to try something and fail than to try nothing and succeed. The result may be the same, but you won't be. We always grow more through defeat than victories.
- Failure doesn't mean you are a failure; it does mean you haven't succeeded.
- Failure doesn't mean you have accomplished nothing; it does mean you have learnt something.

- Failure doesn't mean you have been a fool; it does mean you have a lot of faith.
- Failure doesn't mean you have been disgraced; it does mean you were willing to try.
- Failure doesn't mean you don't have it; it does mean you have to do something in a different way.
- Failure doesn't mean you are inferior; it does mean you are not perfect.
- Failure doesn't mean you will never make it; it just means it will just take a little longer.
- Failure doesn't mean you wasted your life; it does mean you have a reason to start afresh.
- Failure doesn't mean God has abandoned you; it does mean God has a better way.

Consider the following poem:

THE WEAVER

My life is but a weaving
Between my Lord and me,
I cannot choose the colors
He worketh steadily.
Oft times He weaveth sorrow,
And I in foolish pride
Forget He sees the upper
And I, the underside.
Not till the loom is silent
And the shuttles cease to fly
Shall God unroll the canvas
And explain the reason why.
The dark threads are as needful
In the weaver's skilful hand
As the threads of gold and silver
In the pattern He has planned.

Grant Colfax Tullar

Bitter or Better, The Choice Is Yours

Your problems can make you bitter, or they can make you a better person if you choose to learn from them. Nelson Mandela was sent to jail by the oppressive apartheid government of South Africa. After his release 27 years later, he chose to forgive rather than calling for vengeance on those who sent him to jail. Not only that, when he became the president of South Africa, he initiated the Truth and Reconciliation Commission to investigate the wrongs of the past and initiate peace between all those who were wronged and those who wronged them, to heal the wounds and bitterness of the past, and move on to a new, hate-free South Africa. That is the mark of a great leader. Today, he is considered one of the greatest leaders and statesmen of our time.

Fanny Crosby was blind shortly after birth. Yet she did not allow that to stop her. She told herself that she would never allow her handicap to make her bitter. She resolved to develop her potential and make herself a better person who would not be held back by physical disability. That was how the inspiration came to write her first poem at the age of eight:

> *Oh what a happy soul as I*
> *Although I cannot see*
> *I am resolved that in this world*
> *Content I will be.*
>
> *How many blessings I enjoy*
> *That other people don't*
> *To weep and sigh, because I am blind*
> *I cannot, and I would not.*

A positive mental attitude and an indomitable spirit such as Fanny's is always rewarded one way or another. In Fanny's case, her positive attitude towards life generally allowed her to discover early the many gifts that the Lord had blessed her with, particularly poetry and music. In her lifetime, she wrote more than 6,000 hymns, including some of the most famous and best loved Christian songs of all times.

On her 90th birthday, Fanny Crosby said to her friends, "If before birth I had been able to make one request, it would have been that I should be born blind because when I get to heaven, the first face that shall ever gladden my sight would be that of my Saviour Jesus."

Fanny was content and at peace with her situation. How have you managed your own situation? Have you mastered your situation, or have you allowed your situation to cage your potential? Are you still blaming the world for losing a limb in an accident, or have you made peace with your situation and decided to move on with your life and make the most of it despite your situation? Bitter or better – the choice is yours.

It's All in the Way You See Things

Your problem is not the problem. The real problem may be how you see your problem. If you see your problem as a mountain too big to confront, then you have a big problem. On the other hand, if you see your problem as merely a challenge that needs to be broken down and tackled a little at a time, then you are on your way to winning.

A famous writer once said, *The difference between the successful man and the unsuccessful one is not so much a matter of training or equipment. It is not a question of opportunity or luck. It is in the way that each of them look at things.*

There is a huge difference between difficult and impossible. That something is difficult or complicated does not mean it is impossible. A lot of people don't know the difference. To them, whatever needs a lot of complicated steps to get done automatically becomes an impossibility.

An ancient piece of advice for tackling the seemingly impossible is:

Start what is necessary, then what is possible, and suddenly you are going to do the impossible.

Do you see an obstacle as a dead end or as a challenge? That closed door you see may not even be locked. All you have to do is turn the door handle or push a bit harder, and it will open. But most people do not do that. They simply turn back and walk away just because the door is closed.

What you see determines what you get. But what you see may not be all there is. What you think about what you see and what you do about what you see: these determine what you get. One soldier saw a giant on the battlefield and screamed, "This giant is too big to fight." Another soldier saw the same giant and said, "Hey, this target is too big to miss." It depends on your perspective. A teacher raised up an object in class and asked the pupils, "What do you see, kids?" One kid raised up his hand and said, "I see a big hole, Mr. Anderson." Another kid stood up and objected, saying, "I see not just a hole, I see a doughnut, Mr. Anderson."

The story is told about two American men who sat on the porch of their cabin and talked about what they saw as they looked at the lake and miles of beautiful forest before them. The first man shared his vision with his friend:

"I'll tell you what I see when I look out there…I see the underdeveloped resources of northern Minnesota, Wisconsin, and Michigan. I see a syndicated development consortium exploiting over a billion and half dollars in forest products. I see a paper mill and – if the strategic metals are there – a mining operation; a green belt between the condos on the lake and a waste management facility…"

Saying that, he turned to his friend and asked, "Now I ask you, what do you see?"

"I, uh, I just see trees," answered his friend.

What do you see when you look?
- A problem or a challenge?
- A stumbling block or a stepping stone?

- An obstacle or an opportunity?
- A hole or a doughnut?
- A cow pat or fertiliser?
- A vast reserve of untapped resources or just trees?
- A bunch of funny-looking ancestral huts or a major tourist attraction?
- An ugly piece of ancient wood carving or a priceless antique?

It is all in the way you look at things.

Renew Your Mind

The mind works like a computer. It can be programmed and deprogrammed to work in a particular way. What you put in is what you get out. As a man thinks in his heart, so is he (Proverbs 23:7). If the mind has been programmed with negative thoughts, it affects the whole personality. You behave as you have been programmed. You cannot harbour negative thought patterns and expect to act positively. Thoughts produce actions. Actions develop into habits, and habits become character. You always act in consonance with your dominant thought patterns. In other words, you are what you think. That is why you should endeavour to keep your dominant thoughts positive at all times and heed the wise admonition of Mahatma Gandhi and Margaret Thatcher:

Be careful of your thoughts, for your thoughts become your words. Be careful of your words, for your words become your actions. Be careful of your actions, for your actions become your habits. Be careful of your habits, for your habits become your character. Be careful of your character, for your character becomes your destiny.

For you to develop a positive mental attitude, the first thing to do is to lay a new foundation. This new foundation can only be laid after clearing from the mind old negative thought patterns, and laying the underground foundations to support and sustain the new mental structures. These new mental structures are woven together by strands of a positive mental attitude. Retired brain surgeon and former U.S Presidential aspirant, Dr. Ben Carson, once said, "If you take someone with the wrong mindset, you can give them everything in the world and they'll work their way back down to the bottom."

Since a negative mental attitude was learned and accumulated over time, it means that it can also be unlearned and replaced with the right mental attitude, over time. To change our lives, we must change our thoughts. It was Sue Atkinson who said, *"If we change our beliefs and our values we can change our lives."*

To reach your potential and step into the realm of greatness, you must clear all the garbage that has been programmed into you from childhood. Your thought pattern must change from negatives to positives, from defeat to victory, and from "I can't" to "I can." There comes a time in your life when you need to change your mental gear from "It can't be done" to "How to get it done."

By saying, "Yes I can," you release the power of your potential.

By saying, "I can do all things," your creative abilities are stimulated and harnessed.

By saying, "There is always a way," you are motivated to find a way or make one.

By saying, "It is possible," mountains become molehills, problems suddenly change to prospects, and solution channels begin to open.

When you reject the grasshopper mentality, clear the slums of a negative mental attitude and lay new foundations of positive mental structures, impossibilities become possible, new energy surges up within you, and you quickly begin to realise that most of your obstacles are mental in character.

In laying new foundations of healthy mental patterns and cultivating a positive mental attitude, you may want to follow Paul's suggestion to the Philippian Christians (Phil. 4:8), *Whatsoever things are true, whatsoever things are honest, whatsoever things are just, whatsoever things are pure, whatsoever things are lovely, whatsoever things are of good report; if there be any virtue, if there be any praise, think on these things.*

By focusing your thoughts only on things that are true, honest, just, pure, lovely, etc., you are retraining your mind to be attracted to and absorb only that which will nourish and build a healthy, positive and constructive thought pattern.

What You Expect Is What You Get

If you have given up on a situation because you have experienced defeat, it is probably because you have convinced yourself that there is nothing you can do about it. By accepting defeat, you have blocked any avenue through which help can come to you. You have also disconnected your creative energies from the source. Because you have long believed that there is nothing more that you can do to rise from that position of defeat, your mind has gradually accepted the conclusion upon which you have insisted, and when your mind is convinced, you are convinced, for as you think so you are.

But, if on the contrary, you refuse to accept defeat as final and say to yourself: "I can do all things through Christ who strengthens me" (Phil. 4:13), and if you stay with this new positive mental attitude long enough, you will finally convince your own consciousness that there is a way out of your situation. When the mind becomes convinced, nothing becomes impossible, for all things are possible to him who believes (Mark 9:27).

Some psychologists have suggested that if you act as if you are the kind of person you want to be, you will become that person.

If that is the case, then,

- If you act like a winner, you will become a winner.
- If you act confidently, you will become confident.
- If you act like you're already a success, you'll become successful.
- If you act with courage, you will become courageous.
- If you act like you can, you most certainly will.
- And if you keep acting like a loser, you will become a loser.

We are generally motivated to become what we imagine ourselves to be.

You can look at your shortcomings and believe that you can improve.

You can look at your inadequate experience and training and believe that you can acquire new skills.

You can look at your failures and believe that they are not final.

You can look at your weaknesses and believe that they can be corrected, for according to your faith, so shall it be unto you. What you think and believe is what you will become.

If you think you are beaten, you are. If you think you dare not, you don't! If you want to win, but you think you can't, it's almost a cinch you won't. If you think you'll lose, you're lost; for out in the world we find success begins with a fellow's will. It's all in the state of the mind. Life's battles don't always go to the stronger and faster man. But sooner or later the man who wins is the man who thinks he can. (Walter D. Wintle)

POINTS TO PONDER

- The problems you face, the defeats you suffer, and the setbacks you experience can either defeat you or develop you, depending on how you respond to them.
- Success often comes out of failure, and no one who aspires to be great can totally avoid the risk of failure.
- The only way to succeed in life is to take risks – risks that involve the real possibility of failure.
- What one man sees as failure, another man sees as opportunity. What one man sees as impossible, another man sees as a mere challenge that needs to be broken down and tackled piece by piece.
- Greatness in life consists, not only in having a good feeling about success, but also the right attitude towards failure.
- That closed door you see may not even be locked. All you have to do is turn the door handle or push a bit harder, and it will open.
- If you take someone with the wrong mindset, you can give them everything in the world and they'll work their way back down to the bottom.
- Since a negative mental attitude was learned and accumulated over time, it means that it can also be unlearned and replaced with the right mental attitude, over time.

Think truly, and thy thoughts shall the world's famine feed;
Speak truly, and each word of thine shall be a fruitful seed;
Live truly, and thy life shall be a great and noble creed.
Anonymous

APPLICATION ACTIVITIES

1. As you read through this chapter, did you recall some problems you had regarded as impossible to solve because of a wrong mental attitude?

2. If that is the case, make a list of those impossible items. Now for each item on your list, break it down into five different parts. Beginning from the simplest to the most difficult, think carefully and write down at least three things you could do to solve each part of the problem.

3. Now stand back once more and take a look at the original problem. Does it still look impossible to solve?

4. What part of chapter nine meant the most to you?

5. How has this chapter helped to change your attitude towards failure, defeats and temporary setbacks?

Chapter Ten

NEVER GIVE UP!

*Nothing in the world can take the place of persistence.
Talent will not. Nothing is more common than unsuccessful men with
talent.
Genius will not. Unrewarded genius is almost a proverb.
Education will not. The world is full of educated derelicts.
Persistence, determination and hard work make the difference.*
Calvin Coolidge

Winston Churchill was one of the greatest Prime Ministers Britain ever had. He was born on November 30, 1874 and died on January 24, 1965.

When Winston was 12, his father sent him to Harrow School, an English public school for boys situated in Harrow, a part of Greater London. There at Harrow, Winston stayed in the lowest grades three times longer than anyone else. In later life he said, "By being so long in the lowest form (grades) I gained an immense advantage over the clever boys. They all went on to learn Latin and Greek and splendid things like that. But I was taught English. Thus I got into my bones the structure of the ordinary English sentences – which is a noble thing."

During one of his many visits to his old school at Harrow, Sir Winston Churchill was asked to address the students.

Everyone sat still, expecting a flamboyant, eloquent speech from this well-respected orator. But, after the headmaster's profuse introduction of this five-foot-five inches, 107kg intellectual giant, which Churchill graciously acknowledged, he got up and made the following statement that history writers have never been able to get over:

"Young gentlemen, never give up, never give up, never, never, never give up."

Then he sat down. Winston didn't say much on this particular occasion, but many generations later, history still remembers him for those inspiring, fatigue-conquering words he uttered at Harrow.

All successful people have certain things in common: They include persistence, determination to succeed, never accepting failure or defeat as final, and a willingness to try again each time they encounter temporary setbacks. One of such great men who refused to just roll over and play dead at the feet of failure was a former American president and the great slave emancipator, Abraham Lincoln. Born on February 12, 1809 in Kentucky, Abraham Lincoln gained fame as the Great Emancipator largely due to his excellent sense of timing and his open-mindedness. As the 16th president of the United States, Abraham Lincoln helped keep the American Union together during the civil war and abolished slavery in the United States. Remembered for his honesty, compassion, and strength of character, Lincoln remains one of the most respected presidents in American history. But before he became president, he had more than his fair share of failures, painful defeats, and setbacks in life. Lincoln failed in more quests than he succeeded, and lost more elections than he won. But when he finally won, he had proven principles upon which to lead and govern greatly. A close scrutiny of Abraham Lincoln's score sheet shows that he failed in business in 1831. Then he ran for the Legislature in 1832 and was defeated. He went back to business the following year in 1833 and failed again. As if that was not enough, two years later in 1835, his sweetheart died. But that was not the end of his woes, because he suffered a nervous breakdown the following year in 1836. But that did not keep Abraham Lincoln down. He refused to give up and managed to bounce back, and decided to run for office again two years later. Yet again, Lincoln was defeated for speaker in 1838. Anyone else would have given up at this point. Not Abe. He kept on trying, and the more he tried, the more he met with defeats and failures. He was defeated for elector in 1840, defeated for Congress in 1843, and again in 1848. Yet Abraham would not give up. He ran for Senate in 1855 and lost. Then he was defeated again for Vice President in 1856. Abraham Lincoln was defeated for Senate yet again in 1858, before finally, finally, two years later he was elected the President of the United States of America in 1860.

What was it that kept Abraham Lincoln going when anyone else would have given up? How did he bounce back each time he met with failure and defeat? Was there something or someone who was responsible for this indomitable and indefatigable spirit that kept him going? Could it have been a sense of destiny, or some higher power pulling him back up every time he met with failure?

I found a clue to these questions as I began to research more about Abraham Lincoln. It was said of Abraham Lincoln that as a young boy, his dying mother called him to her bedside before passing, and whispered into his ears, "Be somebody Abe." Since a dying man's last words are usually taken very seriously, the young Abe must have taken those last words from his dying mother to heart. Those words must have fired Abraham Lincoln's ambition to be somebody and helped him bounce back every single time in spite of the number of times he had to deal with setbacks and adversity. Abraham Lincoln was a shining example of what a man with an indomitable spirit can achieve. He was able to forge ahead and reach his ultimate goal of becoming president of the United States despite many defeats and painful setbacks in his life. He endured, persevered, and hung in there, never letting go of his goals or his strong resolve to succeed, until at last, he was richly rewarded with success. It was Booker T. Washington who said, *"You measure the size of your accomplishment by the obstacles you had to overcome to reach your goals."*

But why did it take Abraham Lincoln so long to finally reach his goal? He had a vision, he had passion, he was persistent, and he had a never-give-up attitude. Could it be that he was trying to be somebody without defining exactly what he wanted to be? Again, what he said later in his life provides a clue: *"I always wanted to be somebody, but now I realize I should have been more specific."* There it is again – specificity. Have you defined your goal? Is it as specific as possible, or are you still pursuing a general goal? As Zig Ziglar would put it, "Are you a wandering generality, or a meaningful specific?' Have you worked out a plan for bringing your vision into fruition? You will most likely shorten drastically the time it takes you to reach your goal if you follow the goal setting principles provided in this book. But whether or not you succeed at first, don't give up. Keep trying. Abraham Lincoln dared to keep climbing until his dreams came true. You too can climb 'till your dreams come true. The following poem will inspire you to do so:

CLIMB 'TIL YOUR DREAM COMES TRUE

Often your tasks will be many
and more than you think you can do.
Often the road will be rugged
and the hills insurmountable too.

But always remember –
the hills ahead are never as steep as they seem.
And with faith in your heart start upward
and climb 'til you reach your dream.

For nothing in life that is worthy
is ever too hard to achieve
if you have the courage to try it
and you have the faith to believe.

For faith is a force that is greater
than knowledge or power or skill
and many defeats turn to triumph,
if you determine to win you will.

So climb until your dreams come true!

Anonymous

Quitters Never Win

A friend once shared a story of a single mother who was having some problems with her little eight-year-old daughter, Yvonne, who was tired of going to school and was trying to quit. Yvonne thought that schoolwork is hard and the other kids are mean and unkind. Not knowing what to do, the mother took her daughter for counselling. The following conversation ensued between Yvonne and the counsellor:

Yvonne: I don't want to go to school any more.

Counsellor: Why do you say so my child, what's the matter?

Yvonne: Schoolwork is too hard, my friends tease me at school, and Miss Kumar calls me names when I fail to finish her difficult home work.

Carefully pulling Yvonne close to her, and looking lovingly into her tender little eyes, the counsellor continued.

Counsellor: I can understand how you feel my child. I can't blame you for wanting to quit school. But before you finally decide if this is what you really want to do, let me ask you a few questions:

Do you remember Nelson Mandela?

Yvonne: Yes mam.

Counsellor: How about the man called Martin Luther King?

Yvonne: Yes, I remember him.

Counsellor: Fine. Now do you also remember Abraham Lincoln?

Yvonne: Yes, mam, but why are you asking?

Counsellor: I will tell you my child, but first tell me if you remember a man called Alphonsus Stephenson.

After thinking deeply for a while, little Yvonne shook her head and said, "No mam, I don't know him. Who was he?"

Counsellor: That's the point, my child. You don't know him because he gave up on school and quit. People generally don't remember those who quit. So if you refuse to go to school now and quit because of some little problems you are having with your schoolwork, one day, your name will also be mentioned and nobody will remember who you are. Now do you still want to quit and be forgotten, or would you rather hang in there and be remembered as a great person some day?

Yvonne thought for a little while. Then, wiping the little tear drops from the corner of her eyes, she responded with resolve, "No mam. I don't want to quit any more. I want to be great someday."

Counsellor: Good, my child. Now hang in there, do your schoolwork and never, ever give up again. Quitters never win, and winners never quit. Got that?

Yvonne: Yes mam. I got that. Thank you.

And that settled it. Yvonne went home with mum, went back to school and never complained again.

Challenges are like steps of a ladder; every difficult step you take lifts you to a higher level. Those who remain bottom feeders are those who are afraid to take that step. Consider the following poem:

THE ONLY WAY TO WIN

It takes a little courage
and a little self-control,
and some grim determination,
if you want to reach your goal.
It takes a deal of striving
and a firm and stern-set chin,
no matter what the battle,
if you really want to win.

There's no easy path to glory,
there's no rosy road to fame.
Life, however we may view it,
is no simple parlour game;
but its prizes call for fighting,
for endurance and for grit;
for a rugged disposition,
and a don't-know-when-to-quit.

You must take a blow or give one,
You must risk and you must lose,
and expect that in the struggle
you will suffer from the bruise.
But you must not wince or falter
if a fight you once begin;
be a man and face the battle
that's the only way to win.

Poet Unknown

Before success comes in any man's way, he is bound to meet with temporary setbacks and defeat. When a man is overtaken by defeat, the easiest and most logical thing to do is to quit. That is what the majority of people do. Few people succeed because few people are willing to weather the storms and hang in there till victory is won.

> *With ordinary talents and extraordinary courage,*
> *plus faith, perseverance and a 'never-give-up' attitude,*
> *all things are possible, attainable and achievable.*

President Calvin Coolidge, known widely as 'silent Cal,' may not have talked a lot, but when he did say something, it's worth listening to. Here, again, is what he had to say about persistence:

"Nothing in the world can take the place of persistence. Talent will not; nothing is more common than unsuccessful men with talent. Genius will not; the world is full of educated derelicts. Persistence and determination alone are omnipotent. The slogan 'press on' has solved and always will solve the problems of the human race."

Talking about pressing on, there is one man who gets the message loud and clear, and is the epitome of what it means to "press on".

Thomas Alva Edison (1847–1931), was an American inventor whose development of a practical electric light bulb, an electric generating system, a sound-recording device, the film projector, and countless other inventions, has had profound effects on the shaping of modern society. Born in Milan, Ohio, Thomas Edison only had three months of formal education. Yet, he stunned the world with his inventive ingenuity. Thomas Edison is best known for his invention of the electric light bulb. The fact that Edison had numerous successes didn't mean that he was immune to failure. As a matter of fact, Thomas Edison had more failures than anyone else in history. He is said to have failed over 10,000 times while conducting experiments on the light bulb before he finally succeeded. But with each failure, when his assistants asked him why he still continued with these experiments despite repeated failures, he would tell them, "After all, we've discovered one more way that it won't work." What a way to look at failure! No wonder he succeeded at last. If only everyone had the persistence of Edison! He perfectly understood, like William Arthur Ward, that *success is sometimes a series of failures held together by the strong strands of determination and persistence.*

In an article titled *Courage, Brother! There's Still A Little Time!* Reverend Philip S. Barker reflects on the never-give-up persistence of the scientists that makes them winners. He writes:

I am not a scientist, nor have I a scientific turn-of-mind; much less do I understand what makes science, in all its varied and fascinating forms, create the many amazing things it does! But, from the little I know, I have always admired the true scientists' approach to their work.

First, they never allow repeated failure to discourage their rugged and persistent determination to achieve final success, no matter how long success may be delayed. They either persist to the end or they hand over to a younger generation to see the task through for them.

Secondly, they never appear to spend any energy on 'blame' for their many failures and disappointments. They acknowledge humbly their inadequate and incomplete knowledge and press on with courage and undying hope. When one technique fails, enthusiasm is never lacking to try another! "He is not worthy of the honeycomb, that shuns the hive, because the bees have stings" – once wrote the great Shakespeare. In a generation whose moral foundations are being shaken as they have never been shaken before, the great need of the hour is for men of vision, hope, and faith. Men who will disown discouragements, and in spite of formidable odds will face the foe with vigour and flexibility... Life is so demanding and morally critical that none of us have time for little men whose only contribution to life is to find endless reasons and excuses why really great things cannot be done. Or, as the great Bard so succinctly expressed it, "The fault dear Brutus, is not in our stars, but in ourselves that we are underlings." .... So away with littleness, petty meanness, and excuses born of laziness. The need of the day is greatness of heart and mind and action... Victory is assured to the men of courage and persistence, for God is always on the side of the right and the truth, and with His aid in heart and will, we will make this life, yes this human life, the amazing splendour God originally intended.

Success May Just Be Three Feet Away

A story was told of a man who went gold digging during the gold-rush days. After weeks of hard work, he finally struck gold, much more than he was equipped to haul to the surface with his shovel and pickaxe. So he went back home, raised some money to buy machinery, took a few men with him and came back to gather the spoil. After the first car of gold was mined and shipped to the smelter, the returns showed that his days of poverty were over and his life was about to change for ever. A few more shipments would clear his debts and bring him more riches than he could imagine. But all of a sudden, the vein of gold ore disappeared. After several desperate attempts at drilling on to recover the vein, the man and his team gave up their search, packed their equipment and headed home.

Later, the junk man to whom the gold digger had auctioned his equipment brought a mining engineer to examine the gold mine to see if they were right in giving up their search. After looking at the mine with the eyes of an expert and doing a few calculations here and there, the engineer concluded that the vein would be found just three feet from where the gold diggers had stopped drilling.

That was exactly where the gold vein was found – waiting to be discovered. The gold diggers gave up because they knew little about fault lines and failed to seek expert opinion before quitting. This junk man took millions out of this gold mine because someone quit just three feet away from success.

More people fail for lack of persistence than for lack of potential. They have all the potential to succeed but quit when they are just a few feet away from success.

Are you thinking of quitting? Hang in there! Your goldmine may be just a few feet away. Your reward may be just a few steps away. Don't throw away all your labour of love, or sacrifice years of good works because of a fleeting moment of discouragement, because you do not appear to see any visible reward, or because of criticism or ridicule. Remember, *quitters never win, and winners never quit.*

In his encouragement to the Galatian Christians, Paul wrote: *And let us not lose heart and grow weary and faint in acting nobly and doing right, for in due time and at the appointed season we shall reap, if we do not loosen and relax our courage and faint.* (Galatians 6:9 Amp.)

Here, Paul encourages them to keep on acting nobly and doing right. Keeping on, and not giving up is the criteria for winning. Winning happens *in due time and at the appointed season.* This *due time* or *appointed season* could be anything from a few feet away, a few more strikes or a few more trips, right up to a few more days, months or even years. But this *due time*, whenever or whatever it is, shows up only under one condition, namely, *if we do not loosen and relax our courage and faint.* That means that your *due time* will show up only and if you do not give up, quit, or throw in the towel. Only those who persist, endure till the end, keep on keeping on, and refuse to quit, will enjoy the blessings that the due time brings at its coming. Believe me, it is worth waiting for!

The great Confucius said, *"Greatness is not achieved by never failing, but by rising each time we fall. "*

Confucius was right. He was right because statistics have shown that successful people often have more failures in their lives than unsuccessful people. Ask Abraham Lincoln. Thomas Edison can stand on top of the mountain and shout it out loud. He is reputed for conducting over 10,000 unsuccessful experiments before he finally invented the light bulb. With each unsuccessful attempt, he would say to whomever cared to listen, *"I am not discouraged, because every wrong attempt discarded is another step forward. "* That is the right attitude toward success.

Christopher Columbus (1451–1506), was an Italian-Spanish navigator, who sailed west across the Atlantic Ocean in search of a route to Asia, but achieved fame by making landfall instead in the Caribbean Sea. During his voyage to discover what he called the 'New World', the continent that became known as America, he and his men sailed for many days and many nights with no land in sight. As what appeared to be an endless search continued day after day with no land in sight, his sailors became apprehensive and persuaded him repeatedly to cut his losses and turn back. But Christopher Columbus refused to give up and turn back, not even after his sailors threatened mutiny. His mind was set and he was not going to give up halfway. As each day went by, Christopher Columbus strengthened his resolve by entering in the ship's log-book the two words, **'SAIL ON!'**

Rise Up and Try Again

Have you been defeated? Don't just withdraw into your shell or shrink into a corner – with your tail between your legs – and refuse to rise up and try again. Rise up, lick your wounds, and go back 'into the ring'. You are not a failure until you decide to quit. The fact that you've met with temporary defeat does not mean that you can never win. It only means that you need a different tactic, a better plan, some more training, or better timing. Many people experience temporary defeat, then they never want to try again because they keep holding before them the picture of past failures, which create fear and block the way to any future success. If you are one of them, here is good advice for you:

Never allow your past failure to hinder your future success, because the failure of the past could well be the key to your future success.

Here is a poem that will keep you going each time you are tempted to quit:

DON'T QUIT

When things go wrong, as they sometimes will,
When the road you are trudging seems all up hill,
When the funds are low and the debts are high,
And you want to smile, but you have to sigh,
When care is pressing you down a bit,
Rest, if you must – but don't quit.

Life is queer with its twists and turns,
As every one of us sometimes learns,
And many a failure turns about
When he might have won had he stuck it out;
Don't give up, though the pace seems slow –
You might succeed with another blow.

Often the goal is nearer than
It seems to a faint and faltering man,
Often the struggler has given up
When he might have captured the victor's cup.
And he learned too late, when the night slipped down,
How close he was to the golden crown.

Success is failure turned inside out –
The silver tint of the clouds of doubt –
And you never can tell how close you are.
It may be near when it seems far;
So stick to the fight when you're hardest hit –
It's when things seem worst that you musn't quit.

Edgar A. Guest

Don't Give Up

Has your spouse or loved one left you? Have you lost your job, your home, your money, your great opportunity or your health…and now you are even contemplating ending it all? Before you give up, here is a personal testimony of someone who has been exactly where you are and lived to tell the story:

"I quit my job, my relationship, my spirituality…I wanted to quit my life. I went to the woods to have one last talk with God.

'God,' I asked, 'Can you give me one good reason not to quit?'

His answer surprised me…

'Look around,' He said. 'Do you see the fern and the bamboo?'

'Yes,' I replied.

'When I planted the fern and the bamboo seed, I took very good care of them. I gave them light. I gave them water. The fern quickly grew from the earth. Its brilliant green covered the floor. Yet nothing came from the bamboo seed. But I did not quit on the bamboo. In the second year the fern grew more vibrant and plentiful. And again, nothing came from the bamboo seed. But I did not quit on the bamboo', He said.

'In year three there was still nothing from the bamboo seed. But I would not quit. In year four, again there was nothing from the bamboo seed. I would not quit,' He said.

'Then in the fifth year a tiny sprout emerged from the earth. Compared to the fern, it was seemingly small and insignificant. But just six months later the bamboo rose to over 100 feet tall. It has spent the five years growing roots. Those roots made it strong and gave it what it needed to survive. I would not give any of my creations a challenge it could not handle.'

He asked me. 'Did you know, my child, that all this time you have been struggling, you have actually been growing roots?'

'I would not quit on the bamboo. I will never quit on you.'

'Don't compare yourself to others,' He said.

'The bamboo had a different purpose from the fern. Yet they both make the forest beautiful.'

'Your time will come,' God said to me.

'You will rise high.'

'How high should I rise?' I asked.

'How high will the bamboo rise?' He asked in return.

'As high as it can?' I questioned.

'Yes.' He said. 'Give me glory by rising as high as you can.'

I left the forest and brought back this story."

I hope these words can help you see that God will never give up on you. Never give up on yourself, on your dreams, or on life. As long as there is life, there is hope that someday, you too will achieve greatness. Never, never, ever give up!

POINTS TO PONDER

- All successful people have some things in common. They include persistence, determination to succeed, never accepting failure or defeat as final, and a willingness to try again each time they encounter temporary defeat or failure.
- More people fail for lack of persistence than for lack of potential. They have all the potential to succeed, but quit when they are just few feet away from success.
- Only those who persist, endure till the end, keep on keeping on, and refuse to quit, will enjoy the blessings that the *due time* brings at its coming.
- Greatness is not achieved by not failing, but by rising each time we fall.
- With ordinary talents and extraordinary courage, plus faith, perseverance, and a 'never-give-up' attitude, all things are possible, attainable and achievable.
- Never allow your past failure to hinder your future success, because the failure of the past could well be the key to your future success.
- Challenges are like steps of a ladder; every difficult step you take lifts you to a higher level. Those who remain bottom feeders are those who are afraid to take that step.
- When tempted to quit and turn back, remember the words of Christopher Columbus, "SAIL ON!"

> *Great it is to believe the dream*
> *when we stand in youth by the starry stream.*
> *But a greater thing is to fight life through*
> *and say at the end, 'the DREAM is true.'*
> Edwin Markham

APPLICATION ACTIVITIES

1. Write down three important lessons you have learned from this chapter that inspire faith and confidence in you.
2. If you ever come to a point of wanting to give up, what is the one lesson in this chapter that you can hold on to or fall back on to keep you going?
3. Do you know someone around you who has packed up, or is about to pack up and give up on life? With what you now know, how can you help this person, and when?
4. Write down a date and time when you are going to speak to that person.
5. How has this chapter affected your life and your thought patterns? Write down five points.
6. Would you recommend this chapter to someone whom you know to be having a hard time? Yes ☐   No ☐
7. If yes, who and by when?

   a.   Name………………………………………..
        By When…………………………………….

   b.   Name………………………………………..
        By When…………………………………….

   c.   Name………………………………………..
        By When…………………………………….

   d.   Name………………………………………..
        By When…………………………………….

   e.   Name………………………………………..
        By When…………………………………….

NOTES

BIBLIOGRAPHY

CHAPTER ONE
1.   Christian, S. R. (1983) *Alive.* Grand Rapids, Michigan. Zondervan.
2.   Penn, W. (1909-1914) *The Harvard Classics: Some Fruits of Solitude.* New York. P.F. Collier and Song.
3.   Giocondo, Fra Giovanni. (1513) *Within our Reach: Joy.* Letter in the public domain.

CHAPTER TWO
4.   *FAME Weekly* (1994) Whiz Kid Graduates from College At 13. Lagos, Nigeria.

CHAPTER THREE
5.   Broadley Margaret E. (1994) *Your Natural Gifts.* VA, USA. EPM Publications.

CHAPTER FOUR
6.   Reynolds, J. (1769) *Seven Discourses on Art.* Lecture delivered at the Opening of the Royal Academy.
7.   Williams. A. L (1989) *All You Can Do Is All You Can Do But All You Can Do Is Enough!* New York. Random House.

CHAPTER FIVE
8.   *FORTUNE magazine*, January 14th, 1991, pp. 6, 7
9.   *THIS DAY - The Sunday Newspaper*, September 1, 1996. p. 7.

CHAPTER SIX
10.   Hill, N. (2007) *Think and Grow Rich.* (1938). Cleveland, Ohio. The Ralston Society.
11.   *Ebony Magazine.* (1996) Vol LI. (6) Jesse Owens' Olympic Triumph Over Time and Hitlerism. Chicago, Illinois. Johnson Publishing Company.

12. True Story told through E-mail communication AND forwarded by Angelina Sandy, June 27, 2001

CHAPTER SEVEN

13. *The Westminster Collection of Christian Quotations.* Ed. Hanser, M. (2001) Louisville, Kentucky. John Knox Press.

CHAPTER EIGHT

14. Dromgoole, Will A; Dougall, (1966) *The Bridge Builder.* Hugh W. Salt Lake City, UT: The Choir Publishing Co.
15. Hill, N. *The Law of Success.* (1928) Tribeca Books. Meriden, Connecticut. The Ralston Society.
16. Doran, G. T., Miller, A., & Cunningham J. (1981). *There's A S.M.A.R.T. Way To Write Managements' Goals And Objectives.* Management Review, November, 70(11) 35-36.

CHAPTER NINE

17. Maxwell, J. *Failing Forward: Turning Mistakes into Stepping Stones for Success.* (2007) Nashville, Tennessee. Thomas Nelson.

ABOUT THE AUTHOR

Tim Anton Okhai holds a master's degree in clinical engineering from Tshwane University of Technology, Pretoria, South Africa. He is a PhD candidate at University of Paris-Est, France. He is a university lecturer, seminar facilitator and conference speaker who inspires people to be their best by discovering, developing and using their in-built potential to live a life of meaning and purpose. As the International Saline Coordinator for Sub-Saharan Africa, he has travelled extensively in the past few years, training and mentoring different teams in over 30 countries in Africa, Asia, Europe, the Caribbean, the Indian Ocean Islands, and the South Pacific.

He is the founder of Pass to Greatness Foundation, an organization whose mission is to inspire and raise champions who will become instruments of positive change in society, and to help youths in third world countries to strategically position themselves for global impact by maximizing and upscaling their potential for greatness in every sphere of life.

Tim Anton Okhai believes that in your pursuit of greatness, in your quest to be the best at what you do, and in your battle to overcome your limitations and make your dreams come true, "There is always a way – find it!"

If this book has been a blessing to you, please feel free to write a short review on the site where you purchased this book. We would also love to hear from you to know how this book has changed your life. You may contact the author or send your feedback and comments about this book to:

P.O Box, 52104, Saxonwold, GP. 2132
South Africa
WhatsApp: +27 823 424 844
E-mail: passporttogreatness@yahoo.com

www.ingramcontent.com/pod-product-compliance
Lightning Source LLC
Chambersburg PA
CBHW032033050726
47590CB00006B/2392